Battle Of Ia Drang, including: Hal Moore, Battle Of La Drang, We Were Soldiers, We Were Soldiers Once… And Young, Joseph L. Galloway, Bruce P. Crandall, Ed Freeman, Julia Compton Moore

Hephaestus Books

Contents

Articles

References

Hal Moore

Hal Moore

<table>
<tr><th colspan="2">Harold G. Moore</th></tr>
<tr><td colspan="2">Born February 13, 1922</td></tr>
<tr><td colspan="2">
LTG(R) Moore at West Point, 10 May 2010</td></tr>
<tr><td>Nickname</td><td>Hal</td></tr>
<tr><td>Allegiance</td><td>United States of America</td></tr>
<tr><td>Service/branch</td><td>United States Army</td></tr>
<tr><td>Years of service</td><td>1945-1977</td></tr>
<tr><td>Rank</td><td>Lieutenant General</td></tr>
<tr><td>Commands held</td><td>1st Battalion, 7th Cavalry Regiment
7th Infantry Division
Fort Ord Army Training Center
Military Personnel Records Center</td></tr>
<tr><td>Battles/wars</td><td>Korean War
Vietnam War
*Battle of Ia Drang</td></tr>
<tr><td>Awards</td><td>Distinguished Service Cross
Army Distinguished Service Medal
Legion of Merit
Bronze Star (4, of which 2 for valor)
Commendation Medal (2)
Purple Heart
Gallantry Cross (2)</td></tr>
<tr><td>Relations</td><td>Julia Compton Moore</td></tr>
</table>

Other work	Author Executive Vice-President of the Crested Butte Ski Area, Colorado

Harold Gregory "Hal" Moore, Jr. (born February 13, 1922) is a retired lieutenant general in the United States Army and author. Moore is a recipient of the Distinguished Service Cross, which is the second highest military decoration of the United States Army, and was the first of his West Point class (1945) to be promoted to brigadier general, major general, and lieutenant general.

He is best known as the Lieutenant Colonel in command of the 1st Battalion of the 3rd Brigade, 7th Cavalry Regiment, at the Battle of Ia Drang, in 1965 during the Vietnam War; today, he is the "honorary colonel" of the Regiment.

Biography

Born in Bardstown, Kentucky, Moore's chances of obtaining an appointment to West Point were reduced due to the demographics of the area. Moore therefore moved to Washington, D.C., where he completed his high school education, and attended George Washington University for two years before receiving his appointment from a Georgia congressman in 1942 (despite having never before been to Georgia). He graduated from West Point in 1945 and attended graduate studies at George Washington and Harvard universities, obtaining a master's degree in international relations from the latter.

Moore was commissioned as a second lieutenant in 1945. He served with the 187th Airborne Infantry Regiment in Japan from 1945 until 1948. In 1948 he was re-assigned to Fort Bragg. While with the 82nd Airborne Division, he volunteered to join the Airborne Test Section, a special unit testing experimental parachutes, and he made some 150 jumps with the Section over the next two years.

In 1952 Moore was assigned to the 17th Infantry Regiment of the 7th Infantry Division as a Captain in Korean War. While in Korea, he commanded both a rifle company and a heavy mortar company in combat. He next served as Regimental and then Divisional Assistant Chief-of-Staff, Operations and Plans.

In 1954, Moore returned to West Point, this time as a Major, and served for three years as an instructor in infantry tactics. While serving as an instructor at West Point, Moore taught then-Cadet Norman Schwarzkopf, who called Moore one of his "heroes," and cites Moore as the reason he chose the infantry branch upon graduation. Schwarzkopf later became a general and led the UN Coalition forces in the 1991 Gulf War against the Ba'athist Iraq.

Moore next attended the Command and General Staff College, followed by a three-year tour in the Office, Chief of Research and Development where his initiative and insights were key to the development of new airborne equipment and airborne/air assault tactics. Following graduation from the Armed Forces Staff College in 1960 Moore served a three-year tour with Headquarters, Allied Forces Northern Europe in Oslo, Norway.

In 1964, Lieutenant Colonel Moore completed the course of study at the National War College, while earning a master's degree in International Affairs from George Washington University. Moore was transferred to Fort Benning and commanded a battalion in the 11th Air Assault Division, undergoing air assault and air mobility training and tests until July 1965, when the Division was redesignated the 1st Cavalry Division.

Lieutenant Colonel Moore then took his unit: the 1st Battalion, 7th U.S. Cavalry (then in the 3rd Brigade Combat Team, 1st Cavalry Division) to South Vietnam, and led it in the famous Battle of Ia Drang. Encircled by enemy soldiers with no clear landing zone (LZ) that would allow them to leave, Moore managed to persevere despite overwhelming odds that led to a sister battalion only two-and-a-half miles away being massacred. Moore's dictum that "there is always one more thing you can do to increase your odds of success" and the courage of his entire command are credited with this astounding outcome. Importantly, despite the fact that Moore's spirited defense led to more than a 4-to-1 ratio between North Vietnamese casualties and U.S. casualties in their first major engagement of the war, Moore considers the battle a draw because the U.S. forces left the area, allowing the North Vietnamese to reassert control. Many consider this early battle a microcosm of the later war. Moore was known as "Yellow Hair" to his troops at the battle at Ia Drang, for his blonde hair, and as a tongue-in-cheek homage referencing George Armstrong Custer, commander of the same unit (7th Cavalry) at the Battle of the Little Bighorn just under a century before.

After Vietnam, Moore served as Assistant Chief-of-Staff, Operations and Plans of the Eighth Army in South Korea, and Commanding General of the 7th Infantry Division, before rotating back stateside. As Commanding General of the Army Training Center at Fort Ord, California in 1971-1973, he oversaw extensive experimentation in adapting basic and advanced individual training under Project VOLAR in preparation for the end of conscription and the institution of the Modern Volunteer Army. His final assignments took him to the East Coast, as Commanding General of the Military Personnel Records Center, and finally, Deputy Chief of Staff for Personnel, Department of the Army.

After his retirement in 1977, Moore served as the Executive President of the Crested Butte Ski Area, Colorado. In June 2009, the 87-year-old Moore attended the formal opening of the National Infantry Museum in Columbus, Georgia. One of the featured exhibits of the museum is a life-size diorama of LZ X-Ray from the Battle of Ia Drang. In 2010 Moore was a signatory to the "1000+ Flag & General Officers Affirm Law on Gays," which opposes proposed changes in rules concerning gays serving in the US military.

Family

Hal Moore and his deceased wife, Julia Compton Moore, have five children and numerous grandchildren. Two of their sons are career Army officers: one a retired Lieutenant Colonel and another an active duty Colonel.

Books

In 1975, the United States Army Center of Military History published *Building a Volunteer Army: The Fort Ord Contribution*, by Moore and Lieutenant Colonel Jeff M. Tuten. The 139-page paperback is a monograph concerning the Project VOLAR experiments during Moore's tenure in command of Fort Ord in 1971-1973 in preparation for the end of the draft and the implementation of the Modern Volunteer Army.

In 1992 Hal wrote *We Were Soldiers Once… And Young* with co-author Joseph L. Galloway. The book was adapted into the 2002 film *We Were Soldiers*, which was filmed at Forts Benning and Hunter Liggett, depicting Moore's command of 1st Battalion, 7th Cavalry, at Fort Benning and in the Battle of Ia Drang. In the film, Moore was played by Mel Gibson, while Galloway was portrayed by Barry Pepper.

Hal Moore and Joseph L. Galloway have co-authored another book together, a follow-up to their highly successful first collaboration. *We Are Soldiers Still; A Journey Back to the Battlefields of Vietnam* was highly anticipated and published in 2008.

Major awards, decorations and badges

Combat Infantryman Badge (2 awards)

Basic Army Aviator Badge

Master Parachutist Badge (United States)

Original Air Assault Badge

Vietnam Parachutist Badge

Office of the Secretary of Defense Identification Badge

Army Staff Identification Badge

1st Cavalry Division Shoulder Sleeve Insignia

7th Cavalry Regiment

Distinguished Service Cross

Army Distinguished Service Medal

Legion of Merit (with two bronze oak leaf clusters)

Bronze Star (four awards, including two for valor)

Air Medal with one silver and three bronze Oak Leaf Clusters

Joint Service Commendation Medal

Army Commendation Medal (with two bronze oak leaf clusters)

Army Presidential Unit Citation

American Campaign Medal

Asiatic-Pacific Campaign Medal

World War II Victory Medal

Army of Occupation Medal

National Defense Service Medal with one Oak Leaf Cluster

Korean Service Medal with three bronze campaign stars

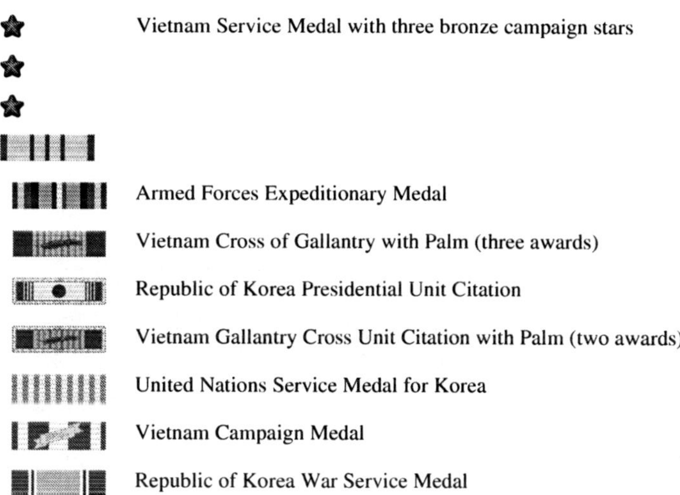

- Order of Saint Maurice by the National Infantry Association
- Distinguished Graduate Award from the West Point Association of Graduates
- Hal Moore is a 2007 recipient of the Joe Ronnie Hooper Award.

External links

- Interview on *We Were Soldiers Once...And Young* [1]
- Interview on *We Are Soldiers Still* [2]
- Gathering of Eagles biography [3]

Battle of la Drang

Battle of la Drang

Battle of Ia Drang Valley	
Part of the Vietnam War	
Bruce P. Crandall's UH-1 Huey unarmed helicopter and U.S. Air Cavalrymen under fire	

Date	November 14–18, 1965
Location	13°35′N 107°43′E Ia Drang Valley, Vietnam
Result	US victory

Belligerents	
North Vietnam Viet Cong	United States South Vietnam
Commanders and leaders	
Nguyễn Hữu An	Thomas W. Brown Harold G. Moore (X-Ray) Robert McDade (Albany)
Strength	
6 infantry battalions (1st and 3rd Battalion, 33rd PAVN Regiment (understrength); 7th, 8th and 9th Battalions, 66th PAVN Regiment; NLF Main Force Battalion H15); separate anti-aircraft and mortar units	3 air cavalry battalions (1st and 2nd Battalions, 3rd Brigade Combat Team; 2nd Battalion, 5th Cavalry Regiment); transport and air and artillery support forces
Casualties and losses	
U.S. estimate: 1,519 killed	304 killed 524 wounded

The **Battle of Ia Drang** was the first major battle between the United States Army and the People's Army of Vietnam (PAVN) (referred to by US fighting units as the North Vietnamese Army (NVA) during the Vietnam War. U.S. CIA agents had been tracking the NVA armies movements since the early fall, and by November 13 U.S. forces had been moved in to attack, backed by artillery equipped with special napalm tipped shells.

The two-part battle took place between November 14 and November 18, 1965, at two landing zones (LZs) northwest of Plei Me in the Central Highlands of South Vietnam (approximately 35 miles south-west of Pleiku). The battle derives its name from the Drang River which runs through the valley northwest of Plei Me, in which the engagement took place. "Ia" means "river" in the local Montagnard language.

Representing the American forces were elements of the 1st Battalion, 7th Cavalry, the 2nd Battalion, and the 5th Cavalry of the United States Army. The North Vietnamese forces included the 66th and 1st battalion/33rd Regiments of the NVA as well National Liberation Front (NLF) (known world wide as the Viet Cong) of the H15 Battalion. The battle featured close air support by U.S. bombers. Both sides suffered heavy losses and both claimed victory. The U.S. lost 234 dead, with 242 wounded; November 17 was the deadliest ambush for Americans in the entire Vietnam War, with 155 men killed and 126 men wounded.

The battle is the subject of the critically acclaimed book *We Were Soldiers Once… And Young* by Harold G. Moore and Joseph L. Galloway. In 2002, Randall Wallace depicted the first part of the battle in the film *We Were Soldiers* starring Mel Gibson and Barry Pepper as Moore and Galloway, respectively. The National Geographic Channel has also aired a program titled "Day Under Fire: Vietnam War" which focuses mainly on the battle of Ia Drang.

Background

Throughout 1963 and 1964 a series of political and military mishaps had seriously affected the capabilities of the Army of the Republic of Vietnam (ARVN) main forces in South Vietnam. ARVN commanders were initially under direct orders by President Ngo Dinh Diem to avoid pitched combat at all costs, allowing the NLF (VC) forces (known around the world as the Viet Cong, or simply "VC") to train and grow without significant opposition, despite losing several leaders to CIA search and destroy squads which relied heavily on rocket attacks using attack helicopters. Even after Diem's overthrow in a 1963 coup, the new military leadership largely consisted of commanders put in place by Diem prior to the coup. They showed equal lack of interest in fighting the NLF, spending their time in a series of coups and counter-coups.

In this vacuum the NLF (VC) units were able to mount increasingly larger military operations. At first these were limited to building up larger formations (battalions and regiments) but by late 1964 they had evolved into an all-out war against ARVN units, which they outperformed in all ways. By early 1965 the majority of rural South Vietnam was under limited VC control, increasingly supported by NVA regulars from North Vietnam. By 1965 ARVN units in the field were hopelessly outclassed and being ambushed and slaughtered.

U.S. advisers in the field had long been pushing for the ARVN forces to be "taken over" by U.S. commanders. In addition to actually getting the men to fight (something they generally seemed willing to do when well-led) the better training and leadership of the U.S. command was expected to be more than enough to make up for the existing deficiencies in the ARVN command. However, the newly-appointed commander of the Vietnam efforts, General William Westmoreland, felt the direct application of U.S. forces was a more appropriate solution; perhaps the ARVN units would not fight, but the same was certainly not true of U.S. Army regulars. By early 1965 he had secured the commitment of upwards of 300,000 U.S. regulars from Lyndon B. Johnson, and was actively trying to get them into the field as soon as possible. Buildup of combat-ready forces took place throughout the summer of 1965.

By 1965, the VC forces were in nominal control of most of the countryside and had set up a major military infrastructure in the Central Highlands, to the northeast of the Saigon region. Vietnamese communist forces had operated in this area during the previous decade in their war against the French, winning a notable victory at the Battle of Mang Yang Pass in 1954. There were few reliable roads into the area, making it an ideal place for the communist forces to form bases that were relatively immune from attack by the generally road-bound ARVN forces. During 1965 large groups of North Vietnamese regulars of the PAVN moved into the area in order to conduct major offensive operations. Attacks to the southwest from these bases threatened to cut South Vietnam in two.

The U.S. command saw this as an ideal area to test their newly developed air mobility tactics. Air mobility called for battalion-sized forces to be delivered into, supplied, and extracted from an area of action using helicopters. Since heavy weapons of a normal combined-arms force could not follow, the infantry would be supported by coordinated air, artillery, and aerial rocket fire arranged from a distance and directed by local observers. They had been practicing these tactics in the U.S. in the newly-created 11th Air Assault Division (Test). The 11th was redesignated the 1st Cavalry Division (the 1st Cavalry had been in South Korea since the Korean War, it was redesignated the 2nd Infantry Division and its colors transferred to the 11th Air Assault (Test) at Ft. Benning Georgia just before deployment overseas.) The division's troopers dubbed themselves the Air Cav. Starting in July 1965 they began deploying to Camp Radcliffe, An Khe, Vietnam. By November most of the division's three brigades were in-field and ready for operations.

In early November 3rd Brigade, 1st Cavalry Division was sent into combat on a search-and-destroy mission in order to track down a force that had unsuccessfully attempted to overrun the Special Forces base at Plei Me, about 25 miles (40 km) south of the 3rd Brigade's base of operations at Pleiku. The 3rd Brigade had searched around the base for several days but had found nothing. Westmoreland sent word to continue the search westwards toward the Cambodian border, but unsure of where to look, the 3rd's commander, Col. Thomas "Tim" Brown, returned to Pleiku in an attempt to gather additional intelligence. He learned of some sort of concentration of forces on Chu Pong Mountain at 13°34′11″N 107°40′54″E, 14 miles (22 km) northwest of Plei Me. Brown decided that this was likely the only lead they had and decided to test the intelligence with a reconnaissance in force.

Landing zones

Brown selected his 1st Battalion, 7th Cavalry, led by Lieutenant Colonel Hal Moore, for the mission, with the explicit orders to not attempt to scale the mountain. There were several clearings in the area that had been designated as possible helicopter landing zones, typically named for a letter of the NATO phonetic alphabet. Moore selected:

- **LZ X-Ray** at 13°34′4.6″N 107°42′50.4″E as his landing zone, a flat clearing surrounded by low trees at the northern base of the Chu Pong Massif and bordered by a dry creek bed on the west. The Ia Drang River was about 2 km to the northwest.
- **LZ Albany** to the north at 13°35′43″N 107°42′55″E
- **LZ Columbus**, just east of Albany at 13°35′20.8″N 107°44′29″E
- **LZ Tango** about 2 km to the north at 13°35′28.8″N 107°42′46″E
- **LZ Yankee** a similar distance south at 13°33′14.1″N 107°43′1.3″E
- **LZ Whiskey**, 2.1 km south-east at 13°33′17.8″N 107°43′40.8″E
- **LZ Victor** at 13°33′33″N 107°43′47.8″E about 4 km to the south-southeast.

Artillery support would be provided from firebase **FB Falcon**, about 8 km to the northeast at 13°37′22″N 107°45′51″E.

X-Ray was approximately the size of a misshapen football field, some 100 meters in length (east to west). It was estimated that only eight Hueys could fit in the clearing at a given time. The 1st/7th was typical for U.S. Army units of the time, consisting of three rifle companies (Alpha through Charlie) and a heavy weapons company (Delta), with about 450 men in total, of the 765 of the battalion's authorized strength. They were to be shuttled by 16 Huey transport helicopters, which could generally carry 10 to 12 equipped troops, so the battalion would have to be delivered in several "lifts" carrying just less than one complete company each time. Each lift would take about 30 minutes. Moore arranged the lifts to deliver Bravo company first, along with his command team, followed by Alpha, Charlie, and finally Delta.

Moore's plan was to move Bravo and Alpha northwest past the creek bed, and Charlie south toward the mountain. Delta Company, which comprised special weapons forces including mortar, recon, and machine gun units, was to be used as the battlefield reserve. In the center of the LZ was a large termite hill that was to become Moore's command post.

1st/7th Cav and the battle for LZ X-Ray

Day 1

1/7 Cavalry at LZ X-Ray

Landings

At 10:48 on November 14, the first elements of Bravo Company of the 1st Battalion/7th Cavalry touched down at LZ X-Ray, following around 30 minutes of bombardment via artillery, aerial rockets, and air strikes. Accompanying Captain John Herren's Bravo Company were Moore and his command group. Instead of attempting to secure the entire landing zone with such a limited force, most of Bravo was kept near the center of the LZ as a strike force, while smaller units were sent out to reconnoiter the surrounding area.

Following their arrival, Herren ordered Alpha to move west past the creek bed. Within approximately 30 minutes, one of his squads under Sergeant John Mingo surprised and captured an unarmed NVA soldier of the 33rd NVA Regiment. The prisoner revealed that there were three North Vietnamese battalions on the Chu Pong Mountain — an estimated 1,600 North Vietnamese troops compared to fewer than 200 American soldiers on the ground at that point.

At 11:20, the second lift of the battalion arrived, with the rest of Bravo Company and one platoon of Alpha Company, commanded by Captain Tony Nadal. At 12:10, the third lift of American forces arrived, consisting of most of Alpha Company. Alpha took up positions to the rear and left flank of Bravo along the dry creek bed, and to the west and to the south facing perpendicular down the creek bed. At 12:15, the first shots were fired on Bravo Company's three platoons that were patrolling the jungle northwest of the dry creek bed. At 12:20, Herren ordered his 1st Platoon under Lieutenant Al Devney and 2nd Platoon under Lieutenant Henry Herrick to advance abreast of each other, and the 3rd (under Lieutenant Dennis Deal) to follow as a reserve unit.

Devney's platoon led approximately 100 yards (91 m) west of the creek bed, with Herrick's men to his rear and right flank. Just before 13:00, Devney's platoon was heavily assaulted on both flanks by the North Vietnamese, taking casualties and becoming pinned down in the process. It was around this point that Herrick radioed in that his men were taking fire from their right flank, and that he was pursuing a squad of communist forces in that direction.

Herrick's platoon is cut off

In pursuit of the North Vietnamese on his right flank, Herrick's platoon was quickly spread out over a space of around 50 meters, and became separated from the rest of the battalion by approximately 100 meters. Soon, Herrick radioed in to ask whether he should enter or circumvent a clearing that his platoon had come across in the bush. Herrick expressed concerns that he might become cut off from the battalion if he tried to skirt the clearing and therefore would be leading his men through it in pursuit of the enemy.

An intense firefight quickly erupted in the clearing; during the first three or four minutes his platoon suffered no casualties and inflicted heavy losses on the North Vietnamese who streamed out of the trees. Herrick soon radioed in that the enemy were closing in around his left and right flanks. Captain Herren responded by ordering Herrick to attempt to link back with Devney's 1st Platoon. Herrick replied that there was a large force between his men and 1st Platoon.

The situation quickly disintegrated for Herrick's 2nd Platoon, which began taking casualties as the North Vietnamese attack persisted. Herrick ordered his men to form a defensive perimeter on a small knoll in the clearing. Within approximately 25 minutes, five men of 2nd Platoon were killed, including Herrick who radioed Herren that he was hit and was passing command over to Sergeant Carl Palmer. Herrick gave vital instructions to his men before he died, including orders to destroy the signals codes and call in artillery support.

Sergeant Ernie Savage assumed command after Sergeant Palmer and Sergeant Robert Stokes were killed. The platoon was technically under the command of Sergeant First Class Mac McHenry, who was positioned elsewhere on the perimeter. Savage assumed command by virtue of being close to the radio and began the process of calling in repeated bombardments of artillery support around the platoon's position. By this point, eight men of 2nd Platoon had been killed and 13 wounded. Under Savage's leadership, and with the extraordinary care of platoon medic Charlie Lose, the men held the knoll for the duration of the battle at X-Ray.

Specialist Galen Bungum of Herrick's Platoon later said of the stand at the knoll:

> “We gathered up all the full magazines we could find and stacked them up in front of us. There was no way we could dig a foxhole. The handle was blown off my entrenching tool and one of my canteens had a hole blown through it. The fire was so heavy that if you tried to raise up to dig you were dead. There was death and destruction all around.[:117,118]”

Sergeant Savage later recalled of the repeated NVA assaults:

> “It seemed like they didn't care how many of them were killed. Some of them were stumbling, walking right into us. Some had their guns slung and were charging bare-handed. I didn't run out of ammo - had about thirty magazines in my pack. And no problems with the M-16. An hour before dark three men walked up on the perimeter. I killed all three of them 15 feet away.[:168]”

Battle for the creek bed

With Herrick's platoon cut off and surrounded, the rest of the battalion fought to maintain a perimeter. At 13:32, Charlie Company under Captain Bob Edwards arrived, taking up positions along the south and southwest facing the mountain.

At around 13:45, through his Operations Officer flying above the battlefield (Captain Matt Dillon), Moore called in air strikes, artillery, and aerial rocket artillery on the mountain to prevent the North Vietnamese from advancing on the battalion's position.

Lieutenant Bob Taft's 3rd Platoon of Alpha Company confronted approximately 150 Vietnamese soldiers advancing down the length and sides of the creek bed (from the south) toward the battalion. 3rd Platoon's troops were told to drop their packs and move forward for the assault. The resulting exchange was particularly costly for 3rd Platoon—its lead forces were quickly cut down. 3rd Platoon was forced to pull back, and Taft was killed. Sergeant Lorenzo Nathan, a Korean War veteran, took command and 3rd Platoon was able to halt the NVA advance down the creek bed.

The NVA forces shifted their attack to 3rd Platoon's right flank in an attempt to flank Bravo. Their advance was quickly stopped by Lieutenant Walter "Joe" Marm's 2nd Platoon (Alpha Company) situated on Bravo's left flank. Moore had ordered Captain Nadal to lend Bravo one of his platoons, in an effort to allow Herren to attempt to fight through to Herrick's position.

From Marm's new position, his men killed some 80 NVA troops with a close range machine gun, rifle, and a grenade assault. The NVA survivors who were not mowed down made their way back to the creek bed, where they were cut down by additional fire from the rest of Alpha Company. Lieutenant Taft's dogtags were discovered on the body of a NVA soldier that had been killed by 3rd Platoon. Upset that Taft's body had been left on the battlefield amidst the chaos, Nadal and his radio operator, Sergeant Jack Gell, brought Taft and the bodies of other Americans back to the creek bed under heavy fire.

Attack from the south

At 14:30 hours, the last troops of Charlie Company arrived, along with the lead elements of Delta Company under Captain Ray Lefebvre. The insertion took place with intense NVA fire pouring into the LZ, and the Huey crews and newly arrived Battalion forces suffered many casualties.

The small contingent of Delta took up position on Alpha's left flank. Charlie Company, assembled along the south and southwest in full strength, was met within minutes by a head-on assault. Edwards radioed in that an estimated 175 to 200 NVA troops were charging his company's lines. With a clear line of sight over their sector of the battlefield, Charlie Company was able to call in and adjust heavy ordnance support with precision, employing the napalm tipped artillery shells, inflicting devastating losses on the Vietnamese forces. Many NVA soldiers were burned to death as they scrambled from their bunkers in a hasty retreaty only to meet a second barrage of artillery shells. as By 15:00 the attack had been quelled, and the NVA ended up withdrawing from the assault approximately one hour after it had been launched.

Attack on Alpha and Delta

At approximately the same time, Alpha and the lead elements of Delta (which had accompanied Alpha at the perimeter in the vicinity of the creek bed) were met by a fierce NVA attack.

Covering the critical left flank from being rolled up by the North Vietnamese were two of Alpha's machine gun crews positioned 75 yards (69 m) southwest of the company's main position. Specialist Theron Ladner (with his assistant gunner Private First Class Rodriguez Rivera) and Specialist 4 Russell Adams (with a-gunner Specialist 4 Bill Beck) had positioned their guns 10 yards (9.1 m) apart, and proceeded to pour heavy fire into the Vietnamese forces attempting to cut into the perimeter between Charlie and Alpha companies. Moore later credited the two gun teams with single-handedly preventing the NVA from rolling up Alpha Company and driving a wedge into the battalion between Alpha and Charlie.

Adams and Rivera were severely wounded in the onslaught. After the two were carried to the battalion's collection point at Moore's command post to await evacuation by air, Beck, Ladner, and Private First Class Edward Dougherty (an ammo-bearer) continued their close range suppression of the Vietnamese advance.

Beck later said of the battle:

> When Doc Nall was there with me, working on Russell, fear, real fear, hit me. Fear like I had never known before. Fear comes, and once you recognize it and accept it, it passes just as fast as it comes, and you don't really think about it anymore. You just do what you have to do, but you learn the real meaning of fear and life and death. For the next two hours I was alone on that gun, shooting at the enemy.[:133]

Delta's troops also experienced heavy losses in repelling the NVA assault, and Captain Lefebvre was wounded soon after arriving to X-Ray. One of his platoon leaders, Lieutenant Raul Taboada was also severely wounded, and Lefebvre passed command to Staff Sergeant George Gonzales (who, unknown to Lefebvre, had also been wounded).

While medical evacuation helicopters (medevacs) were supposed to transport the battalion's growing casualties, only two were evacuated by medevacs before the pilots called off their mission under intense fire from the NVA. Casualties were loaded onto the assault Hueys (lifting the battalion's forces to X-Ray), whose pilots carried load after load of wounded from the battlefield. Battalion intelligence officer Captain Tom Metsker (who had been wounded) was fatally hit when helping his wounded comrade Ray Lefebvre aboard a Huey.

360-degree perimeter

Captain Edwards ordered Sergeant Gonzales to position Delta Company on Charlie's left flank, extending the perimeter to cover the southeast side of X-Ray.

At 15:20, the last of the battalion arrived, and Lieutenant Larry Litton assumed command of Delta. It was during this lift that one Huey, having approached the LZ too high, crash-landed on the outskirts of the perimeter near the command post (those on board were quickly rescued by the battalion).

With Delta's weapons teams on the ground, its mortar units were massed with the rest of the battalion's in a single station to support Alpha and Bravo. Delta's reconnaissance platoon (commanded by Lieutenant James Rackstraw) was positioned along the north and east of the LZ, establishing a 360-degree perimeter over X-Ray. Had the NVA forces circled around to the north of the U.S. positions prior to this point, they would have found their approach unhindered.

Second push to the lost platoon

As the NVA attack on Alpha Company diminished, Moore organized for another effort to rescue Herrick's lost platoon. At 15:45, Moore ordered Alpha and Bravo to evacuate their casualties and pull back from engagement with the enemy.

Shortly after, Alpha and Bravo began their advance toward Herrick's lost platoon from the creek bed. The force quickly suffered casualties. At one point, Bravo's advance was halted by a firmly entrenched North Vietnamese machine gun position at a large termite hill. After firing a light anti-tank weapon (LAW) into it with no effect, Lieutenant Marm attacked the position single-handedly. Under fire, Marm charged the Vietnamese gun, eliminating it with grenade and rifle fire. The following day, a dozen dead NVA troops (including one officer) were found in the position. Marm was wounded in the neck and jaw in the assault and was later awarded the Medal of Honor for his lone assault.

The second push had advanced just over 75 yards (69 m) toward the lost platoon's position before reaching a stalemate with the NVA. At one point, the NVA were firing on Alpha's 1st Platoon (which was leading the advance and was at risk of becoming separated from the battalion) with an American M-60 machine gun that had been taken off a dead gunner of Herrick's platoon. The stalemate lasted between 20 and 30 minutes before Nadal and Herren requested permission to withdraw back to X-Ray (to which Moore agreed).

Americans dig in for the night

Near 17:00 hours the lead elements of Bravo Company of the 2nd Battalion/7th Cavalry (the "sister battalion" of the 1st/7th under Moore) arrived at LZ X-Ray to reinforce the embattled battalion. In preparation for a defensive position to last the night, Moore ordered Bravo's (2nd/7th) commander Captain Myron Diduryk to place two of his platoons between Bravo (1st/7th) and Delta on the northeast side of the perimeter. Diduryk's 2nd Platoon was used to reinforce Charlie Company's position (which was stretched over a disproportionately long line).

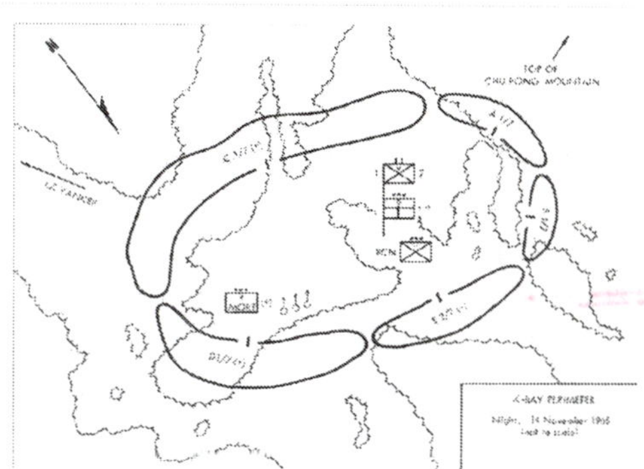

Situation during the night of November 14

By nightfall, the battle had taken a heavy toll on Moore's battalion. Bravo had taken 47 casualties (including one officer), and Alpha had taken 34 casualties (including three officers). Charlie Company was comparatively healthy (having taken only four casualties).

The American forces were placed on full alert throughout the night. Under the light of a bright moon, the Vietnamese probed every company on the perimeter (with the exception of Delta) in small squad-sized units. The Americans exercised some level of restraint in their response. The M-60 gun crews, tactically positioned around the perimeter to provide for multiple fields of fire, were told to hold their fire until otherwise ordered (so as to conceal their true location from the NVA).

The lost platoon under Sergeant Savage's command suffered three sizable assaults of the night (one just before midnight, one at 03:15, and one at 04:30). The NVA, using bugles to signal their forces, were repelled from the knoll with artillery, grenade, and rifle fire. The lost platoon survived the night without taking additional casualties.

Day two

Attack at dawn

Just before dawn at 06:20, Moore ordered his companies to put out reconnaissance patrols to probe for North Vietnamese forces.

At 06:50, patrols from Charlie Company's 1st Platoon (under Lieutenant Neil Kroger) and 2nd Platoon (under Lieutenant John Geoghegan) had advanced 150 yards (140 m) from the perimeter before coming into contact with NVA troops. A firefight broke out, and the patrols quickly withdrew to the perimeter.

Shortly after, an estimated 200-plus North Vietnamese troops charged 1st and 2nd platoons on the south side of the perimeter. Heavy ordnance support was called in, but the NVA were soon within 75 yards (69 m) of the battalion's lines. Their fire began to cut through Charlie Company's positions and into the command post and the American lines across the LZ.

1st and 2nd platoons suffered significant casualties in this assault, including Kroger and Geoghegan. Geoghegan was killed while attempting to rescue one of his wounded men, Private First Class Willie Godboldt (who died of his wounds shortly thereafter). Two M-60 crews (under Specialist James Comer and Specialist 4 Clinton Poley, Specialist 4 Nathaniel Byrd, and Specialist 4 George Foxe) were instrumental in suppressing the North Vietnamese advance from completely overrunning Geoghegan's lines.

Following this attack, Charlie's 3rd Platoon was soon met with a NVA assault. Captain Edwards was wounded, and Lieutenant John Arrington assumed command of the company (and was quickly wounded).

Three-pronged attack

At 07:45, the NVA launched an assault on Crack Rock, near its connection with the beleaguered Charlie Company. Fire started to penetrate the battalion command post, which suffered several wounded (including Moore's own radio operator, Specialist 4 Robert Ouellette).

Under heavy attack on three sides, the battalion fought off repeated waves of PAVN infantry. It was during this battle that Specialist Willard Parish of Charlie Company, situated on Delta's lines, earned a Silver Star for suppressing an intense Vietnamese assault in his sector. After expending his M-60 ammunition, Parish resorted to his .45 sidearm to repel NVA forces that advanced within 20 yards (18 m) of his foxhole. After the battle, over 100 dead North Vietnamese troops were discovered around Parish's position.

As the battle along the southern line intensified, Lieutenant Charlie W. Hastings (*USAF liaison: forward air controller*), made the decision (based on criteria established by the USAF) to transmit the code phrase "Broken Arrow", which relayed that an American combat unit was in danger of being overrun. In so doing, Hastings was calling on all available support aircraft in the country to come to the battalion's defense, drawing on a significant arsenal of heavy ordnance support.

On Charlie Company's broken lines, NVA troops walked the lines for several minutes, killing wounded Americans and stripping their bodies of weapons and other items. It was around this time, at 07:55, that Moore ordered his lines to throw colored smoke grenades over the lines to identify the battalion's perimeter. Aerial fire support was then called in on the NVA at close range — including those along Charlie Company's lines.

Shortly after, Moore's command post was subjected to what could have been a catastrophic friendly fire incident. Two F-100 Super Sabre jets approached X-Ray, the first dropping napalm inadvertently on American lines, the second approaching the command post in a similar manner. The command post was saved when Hastings frantically radioed for the second jet to change course. Despite Hastings' best efforts, several Americans were wounded and killed by this air strike.

Attack ends

At 09:10, the first elements of Alpha Company of the 2nd Battalion of the 7th Cavalry under Captain Joel Sugdinis arrived at X-Ray. Sugdinis' forces reinforced the remains of Charlie Company's lines.

By 10:00, the North Vietnamese had begun to withdraw from the battle — although occasional fire continued to harass the battalion. Charlie Company, having inflicted scores of losses on the NVA, had suffered 42 Killed in action (KIA) and 20 Wounded in action (WIA) over the course of the two-and-a-half-hour assault. Lieutenant Rick Rescorla of Diduryk's Bravo Company, who later died in the September 11th attacks on the World Trade Center, later remarked after having policed up the battlefield in Charlie Company's sector following the assaults:

> There were American and NVA bodies everywhere. My area was where Lieutenant Geoghegan's platoon had been. There were several dead NVA around his platoon command post. One dead trooper was locked in contact with a dead NVA, hands around the enemy's throat. There were two troopers — one black, one Hispanic — linked tight together. It looked like they had died trying to help each other.:215

Reinforcements

Given the tempo of combat at LZ X-Ray and the losses being suffered, other units of the 1st Cavalry Division planned to land nearby and then move overland to X-Ray. The 2nd Battalion of the 5th Cavalry was to be flown into LZ Victor, about 3.5 kilometers east-southeast of LZ X-Ray. They flew in at 08:00 and quickly organized to move out, the trip taking about 4 hours. Most of this was uneventful until they were approaching X-Ray. At about 10:00, some 800 yards (730 m) to the east of the LZ, the 2nd/7th's Alpha company received some light fire and had to set up a combat front. At 12:05, Tully's forces had arrived at the LZ.

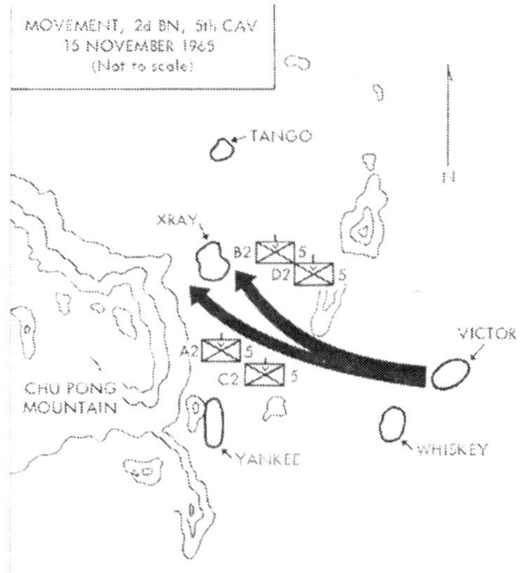

Relief of LZ X-Ray on November 15th

Third push to the lost platoon

Using a plan devised by Moore, Tully commanded Bravo/1st/7th and his own Alpha/2nd/5th and Charlie/2nd/5th companies in a third major effort to relieve the lost platoon under Sergeant Ernie Savage. Making use of fire support, the relief force slowly but successfully made its way to the knoll without encountering NVA elements. 2nd Platoon had survived but at a significant cost; out of the 29 men, nine were KIA and a further 13 WIA. At around 15:30, the relief force began to encounter sniper fire and began the process of carrying the wounded and dead of the lost platoon back to X-Ray.

The expanded force at X-Ray, consisting of Moore's weakened 1st Battalion of the 7th, Tully's 2nd Battalion of the 5th, and one company of the 2nd Battalion of the 7th consolidated at X-Ray for the night. At the LZ, the wounded and dead were evacuated, and the remaining American forces dug in and fortified their lines.

Second night

While the American lines at X-Ray were harassed at various times during the night by PAVN probes, it was shortly before 04:00 that grenade booby traps and trip flares set by Captain Diduryk's Bravo Company began to erupt. At 04:22, the NVA launched a fierce assault against Diduryk's men.

Bravo fought off this attack by an estimated 300 NVA in minutes. A decisive factor in this stand, in addition to rifle and machine gun fire from Bravo's lines, was the skilled placement of artillery strikes by Diduryk's forward observer, Lieutenant Bill Lund. Making use of four different artillery batteries, Lund organized fire into separate concentrations along the battlefield, with devastating consequences for the waves of advancing NVA.

The NVA repeated their assault on Diduryk's lines some 20 minutes after the first, as flares dropped from American C-123 Provider aircraft flying above illuminated the battlefield to Bravo's advantage. For around 30 minutes, Bravo fought off the NVA advance with a combination of small arms and Lund's skilled organization of artillery strikes.

Shortly after 05:00, a third attack was launched against Diduryk's forces, which was repelled by Lieutenant James Lane's platoon within 30 minutes.

At almost 06:30, the NVA launched yet another attack on Diduryk's men — this time in the vicinity of the company command post. Again, Lund's precision in ordering artillery strikes cut down scores of NVA forces, while Diduryk's men repelled those who survived with rifle and machine gun fire.

At the end of these attacks, with daybreak approaching, Diduryk's Bravo Company had only six lightly wounded among its ranks — with none killed.

LZ X-Ray secured

By the morning of November 16, the 1st Battalion, 7th Cavalry had been reinforced by the remaining elements of 2nd Battalion, 7th Cavalry and 2nd Battalion, 5th Cavalry. Unattrited this would have put the U.S. forces on rough parity with the original NVA forces, three battalions, or about one complete brigade each. That afternoon, 1st/7th Cav. withdrew from the battle zone while the 2nd/7th Cav. and 2nd/5th Cav. took up defensive positions for the night.

The battle was ostensibly over. The NVA forces had suffered thousands of casualties and were no longer capable of a fight. U.S. forces had suffered 79 killed and 121 injured and had been reinforced to levels that would guarantee their safety. Given the situation there was no reason for the U.S. forces to stay in the field, their mission was complete and arguably a success. Moreover, Col. Brown, in overall command, was worried about reports that additional PAVN units were moving into the area over the border. He wanted to withdraw the units, but General Westmoreland demanded that the 2nd/7th Cav. and 1st/5th Cav stay at X-Ray in order to avoid the appearance of a retreat.

2nd/7th Cav and the ambush near LZ Albany

The next day, the two remaining battalions abandoned LZ X-Ray and began a tactical march to new landing zones, 2nd/5th under Lt. Col. Bob Tully to LZ Columbus about 4 km to the northeast, and 2nd/7th under Lt. Col. Robert McDade to LZ Albany about 4 km to the north-northeast, close to the Ia Drang. Air Force B-52 Stratofortresses were on their way from Guam, and their target was the slopes of the Chu Pong massif. The U.S. ground forces had to move outside a two-mile (3 km) safety zone by midmorning to be clear of the bombardment. Tully's men moved out at 09:00; McDade's followed ten minutes later.[:277,278]

Events leading to the ambush

The first indication of enemy presence was observed by the point units of the American column, the point squad of the reconnaissance platoon under Staff Sergeant Donald J. Slovak, who saw "Ho Chi Minh sandal foot markings, bamboo arrows on the ground pointing north, matted grass and grains of rice".[:285,286] After marching about 2,000 meters, Alpha Company leading the 2nd/7th headed northwest, while the 2nd/5th continued on to LZ Columbus. Alpha Company came upon some grass huts which they were directed to burn. At 11:38, Bob Tully's men, the 2nd/5th, were logged into its objective, LZ Columbus.

Communist troops in the area consisted of the 8th Battalion, 66th Regiment, the 1st Battalion 33rd Regiment, and the headquarters of the 3rd Battalion, 33rd Regiment, of the NVA. While the 33rd Regiment's battalions were understrength from casualties incurred during the battle at the Special Forces Plei Me camp, the 8th was General An's reserve battalion, fresh and rested.[:288]

Alpha Company soon noticed the sudden absence of air cover and their commander, Captain Joel Sugdinis wondered where the ARA choppers were. He soon heard the sound of distant explosions to his rear; the B-52's were making their bombing runs on the Chu Pong massif.

Lieutenant D. P. (Pat) Payne, the recon platoon leader, was walking around some termite hills when he suddenly came upon a North Vietnamese soldier resting on the ground. Payne jumped on the NVA trooper and took him prisoner. Simultaneously, about ten yards away, his platoon sergeant captured a second NVA soldier. Other members of the NVA recon team may have escaped and reported to the headquarters of the 1st Battalion, 33rd Regiment. The North Vietnamese then began to organize an assault on the American column. As word of the capture reached him, Lt. Col. McDade ordered a halt as he went forward from the rear of the column to interrogate the prisoners personally. The POW's were policed up about a hundred yards from the southwestern edge of the clearing called Albany, the report of which reached division forward at Pleiku at 11:57.[:289,290]

McDade then called his company commanders forward for a conference; most of whom were accompanied by their radio operators. Alpha Company moved forward to LZ Albany; McDade and his command group were with them. Following orders, the other company commanders were moving forward to join McDade. Delta Company, which was next in the column following Alpha Company, was holding in place; so was Charlie Company which was next in line. Battalion Headquarters Company followed, and Alpha Company of the 1st Battalion, 5th Cavalry brought up the rear of the column. The American column was halted in unprepared, open terrain,and strung out in 550-yard (500 m) line of march.[:292,293] Most of the units had flank security posted, but the men were worn out from almost sixty hours without sleep and four hours of marching. The elephant grass was chest-high so visibility was limited. The column's radios for air or artillery support were with the company commanders.

Contact

An hour and ten minutes after the NVA recon soldiers were captured, Alpha Company and McDade's command group had reached the Albany clearing. McDade and his group walked across the clearing and into a clump of trees. Beyond that clump of trees was another clearing. The remainder of the battalion was in a dispersed column to the east of the LZ. Battalion Sergeant Major James Scott and Sergeant Charles Bass then attempted to question the prisoners again. While they were doing this, Bass heard Vietnamese voices, and the interpreter confirmed that these were NVA talking. Alpha Company had been in the LZ about five minutes. Right about then, small arms fire erupted.

Lt. Pat Payne's reconnaissance platoon had walked to within 200 yards (180 m) of the headquarters of the 3rd Battalion, 33rd Regiment; the 550-man strong 8th Battalion, 66th Regiment had been bivouacked off to the northeast of the American column. As the Americans rested in the tall grass, North Vietnamese soldiers were swarming towards them by the hundreds. It was 13:15. The close quarters, intense battle lasted for sixteen hours.[:293-295]

Ambush

The North Vietnamese forces first struck at the head of the 2nd Battalion column and rapidly spread down the right or east side of the column in what appears to be an L-shaped ambush. NVA troops ran down the length of the column, with units peeling off to attack the outnumbered Americans, engaging in intense, brutal close-range and hand-to-hand combat.

McDade's command group made it into the clump of trees between the two clearings that constituted LZ Albany. They took cover from rifle and mortar fire within the trees and termite hills. The recon platoon and the Alpha Company 1st Platoon provided initial defense at the position. By 13:26, they had been cut off from the rest of the column; the area from whence they had come was swarming with NVA soldiers. While they waited for air support, the Americans holding Albany drove off assaults by

NVA troopers and sniped at the exposed enemy wandering around the perimeter. It was later discovered that North Vietnamese were mopping up, looking for Americans wounded in the tall grass and killing them.[:300-305]

All the while the noise of battle could be heard in the woods as the other companies fought for their lives. Charlie and Alpha companies lost a combined 70 men in the first minutes; Charlie Company suffered 45 dead and more than 50 wounded, the heaviest casualties of any unit that fought on Albany.[:309] Air Force A-1E Skyraiders soon provided much-needed support, dropping napalm. However, because of the fog of war and the inter-mixing of both American and North Vietnamese troops, it is likely that the air and artillery strikes killed not just NVA, but Americans as well.

The 2nd Battalion, 7th Cavalry had been reduced to a small perimeter at Albany composed of survivors of Alpha Company, the recon platoon, survivors from the decimated Charlie and Delta Companies and the command group. There was also a smaller perimeter at the rear of the column about 500-700 yards due south: Captain George Forrest's Alpha Company, 1st Battalion, 5th Cavalry. Captain Forrest had run a gauntlet all the way from the conference called by McDade back to his company when the NVA mortars started coming in.

American reinforcements arrive

At 14:55, Bravo Company, 1st Battalion, 5th Cavalry under Captain Buse Tully began marching from LZ Columbus to the rear of the 2nd Battalion, 7th Cavalry column that was about two miles (3 km) away. By 16:30, they came into contact with the Alpha Company perimeter under Captain Forrest. A one-helicopter landing zone was secured, and the wounded were evacuated. Captain Tully's men then began to push forward towards where the rest of the ambushed column would be. PAVN troopers contested their advance, and the Americans came under fire from a wood line. Tully's men assaulted the tree line and drove off the North Vietnamese. At 18:25, orders were received to secure into a two-company perimeter for the night. They planned to resume the advance at daybreak.[:339,340]

At around 16:00, Captain Myron Diduryk's Bravo Company, 2nd Battalion, 7th Cavalry, veterans of the fight at LZ X-Ray, got the word that they would be deployed in the Battalion's relief. At 18:45 the first lift ships swept over the Albany clearing and the troopers deployed into the tall grass.[:341-343] Lieutenant Rick Rescorla, the sole remaining platoon leader in Bravo Company, led the reinforcements into the Albany perimeter, which was expanded to provide better security. The wounded at Albany were evacuated at around 22:30 that evening, the ships receiving intense ground fire as they landed and took off. The Americans at Albany then settled down for the night.

The next day, Friday, November 18 dawned on the battlefield. The Americans began to police up their dead. This task took the better part of the day and the next. American and North Vietnamese dead were scattered all over the field of battle. Rescorla described the scene as, "a long, bloody traffic accident in the jungle."[:369] While policing the battlefield, Rescorla recovered a large, battered, old French army bugle from a dying NVA soldier. The Americans finally left Albany for LZ Crooks at 13°40′5.6″N

107°39′10″E, six miles (10 km) away, on November 19.

The battle at LZ Albany cost the Americans 155 men killed and 124 wounded.[:295] One American, Toby Braveboy, was recovered on November 24 when he waved down a passing H-13 scout helicopter.[:352-354]

Aftermath

This battle can be seen as a blueprint for tactics by both sides. The Americans used air mobility, artillery fire and close air support to accomplish battlefield objectives. The NVA and Viet Cong forces learned that they could neutralize that firepower by quickly engaging American forces at very close range. The North Vietnamese commander, General Nguyen Huu An, included his lessons from the battle at X-ray in his orders for Albany, "Move inside the column, grab them by the belt, and thus avoid casualties from the artillery and air." Both Westmoreland and General An thought this battle to be a success. In November 1965 the NVA thrust to split South Vietnam in two had been defeated.

Casualty notification

The U.S. Army had not yet set up casualty-notification teams this early in the war. The notification telegrams at this time were handed over to taxi cab drivers for delivery to the next of kin. Hal Moore's wife, Julia Compton Moore, followed in the wake of the deliveries to widows in the Ft. Benning housing complex, grieving with the wives and comforting the children, and attended the funerals of all the men killed under her husband's command who were buried at Fort Benning. Her complaints about the notifications prompted the Army to quickly set up two-man teams to deliver them, consisting of an officer and a chaplain.

Mrs. Frank Henry, the wife of the battalion executive officer, and Mrs. James Scott, wife of the battalion command sergeant major, performed the same duty for the dead of the 2nd Battalion, 7th Cavalry.[:416]

Notable Awards

Second Lieutenant Walter Marm (later Colonel) received the Medal of Honor on 15 February 1967 for his actions during the 3-day battle at LZ X-Ray. His MOH citation recounts several examples of conspicuous gallantry, some despite being severely wounded.

On February 26, 2007, helicopter pilots Major Bruce Crandall (later Lieutenant Colonel) and Captain Ed Freeman (later Major) were each awarded the Medal of Honor for their numerous volunteer flights (22 and 14, respectively) into LZ X-Ray while enemy fire was so heavy that medical evacuation helicopters refused to approach. With each flight, Crandall and Freeman delivered much needed water and ammunition and extracted wounded soldiers, saving countless lives.

Lieutenant Colonel Harold "Hal" Moore (later Lieutenant General), Commanding Officer, 1st Battalion, 7/1 U.S. Cavalry (Airmobile) was awarded the Distinguished Service Cross for his actions at LZ X-Ray. His DSC citation particularly commends his "leadership by example" as well as his skill in battle against overwhelming odds and his unwavering courage.

Journalist Joseph Galloway would be the only civilian awarded the Bronze Star Medal for valor for actions in Vietnam. Taking up arms alongside the overwhelmed men he was covering, he repeatedly disregarded his own safety to rescue wounded soldiers under fire.

Although many notable decorations have been awarded to veterans of the Battle of Ia Drang, in his book "We Were Soldiers Once...And Young", LTG Moore writes:

> "We had problems on the awards... Too many men had died bravely and heroically, while the men who had witnessed their deeds had also been killed... Acts of valor that, on other fields, on other days, would have been rewarded with the Medal of Honor or Distinguished Service Cross or a Silver Star were recognized only with a telegram saying, 'The Secretary of the Army regrets...' The same was true of our sister battalion, the 2nd of the 7th."

See also

- *We Were Soldiers*
- *We Were Soldiers Once ... And Young*
- Joseph L. Galloway
- Jim H. Clary
- Bruce P. Crandall
- Ed Freeman
- Chickenhawk (book)
- Robert Mason (writer)
- Rick Rescorla

Further reading

- Cash, John A.; Albright, John; Sandstrum, Allan W. (1985 (reissue from 1970)). "1. Fight at Ia Drang" [1]. *Seven Firefights in Vietnam* [2]. The United States Army Center of Military History.
- Moore, Hal G.; Galloway, Joseph L.. *We were soldiers once... and young* (5th ed.). ISBN 0679411585.

External links

- LZ X-Ray [3]
- OPERATION SILVER BAYONET: THE BATTLE OF THE IA DRANG [4]
- Rescue at LZ Albany [5]

- Major Bruce P.Crandall - Medal of Honor for actions at LZX-Ray [6]
- Captain Ed W. Freeman - Medal of Honor for actions at LZ X-Ray [7]
- 2nd Lieutenant Walter J. Marm Jr. - Medal of Honor for actions at LZ X-Ray [8]
- Jack Smith's account of the battle [9]

We Were Soldiers

We Were Soldiers

We Were Soldiers	
Theatrical release poster	
Directed by	Randall Wallace
Produced by	Arne L. Schmidt Jim Lemley Randall Wallace
Written by	Hal Moore Joseph L. Galloway (book) Randall Wallace (screenplay)
Starring	Mel Gibson Madeleine Stowe Sam Elliott Greg Kinnear Chris Klein Keri Russell Barry Pepper
Studio	Icon Productions
Distributed by	Paramount Pictures (US) Icon Film Distribution (International)
Release date(s)	March 1, 2002
Running time	138 minutes
Country	United States
Language	English French Vietnamese
Budget	$75 million
Gross revenue	$114,660,784

We Were Soldiers is a 2002 American war film that dramatized the Battle of Ia Drang on November 14, 1965 — the first major engagement of the United States Army in the Vietnam War. The film was directed by Randall Wallace and stars Mel Gibson. It is based on the book *We Were Soldiers Once… And Young* by Lieutenant General (Ret.) Hal Moore and reporter Joseph L. Galloway, both of whom were at the battle.

Plot

A French Army unit is on patrol in Vietnam in 1954 during the First Indochina War. The captain of the patrol curses the land when they see nothing. Then, the unit is suddenly ambushed by Vietminh forces who kill the officers and, although the unit kills many NVA it is eventually overrun. Nguyen Huu An, hypothesising that if they take no prisoners the French will eventually stop sending troops, orders the execution of all surviving French soldiers.

Eleven years later, Lieutenant Colonel Hal Moore (Mel Gibson), a dedicated U.S. soldier, is deeply committed to training his troops, who are preparing to be sent to Vietnam. The night before their departure, the unit's officers hold a party to celebrate. Moore learns from a superior officer that his unit will be known as the 1st Battalion / 7th cavalry regiment. He is disquieted because the 7th Cavalry regiment was the unit commanded by General George Custer in the 19th Century when he and his men were slaughtered at the Battle of the Little Bighorn. Moore is also dismayed because President Lyndon B. Johnson has decreed that the war would be fought "on the cheap," without declaring it a national emergency. As a result, Moore believes he will be deprived of his oldest, best-trained soldiers (a formal declaration of war would have meant mobilization and extension of the terms of enlistment for volunteer soldiers) - about 25% of his battalion - just prior to shipping out for Vietnam. Before leaving for Vietnam, Moore delivers a touching speech to his unit:

"Look around you, in the 7th Cavalry, we got a Captain from the Ukraine, another from Puerto Rico, we got Japanese, Chinese, Blacks, Hispanics, Cherokee Indian, Jews and Gentiles, all American. Now here in the States some men in this unit may experience discrimination because of race or creed, but for you and me now, all that is gone. We're moving into the valley of the shadow of death, where you will watch the back of the man next to you, as he will watch yours, and you won't care what color he is or by what name he calls God. Let us understand the situation; we're going into battle against a tough and determined enemy. I can't promise you that I will bring you all home alive, but this I swear: when we go into battle, I will be the first one to set foot on the field, and I will be the last to step off. And I will leave no one behind. Dead or alive, we will all come home together. So help me God."

After arriving in Vietnam, he learns that an American base has been attacked, and is ordered to take his 400 men after the enemy and eliminate them, despite the fact that intelligence has no idea of the number of enemy troops. He leads a newly created air cavalry unit into the Ia Drang Valley against over 4,000 -6,000 well equipped enemy soldiers.

An emotional toll is taken back home, where Moore's wife Julie (Madeleine Stowe) and another soldier's wife take over the job of delivering telegrams that inform families (mainly wives like themselves) living at Fort Benning, Georgia, the unit's base of operation, of soldiers' deaths.

After landing in the "Valley of Death", the soldiers capture a North Vietnamese Army lookout who informs them that the location they were sent to is actually the Base camp of an entire North Vietnamese Army division over 4,000 men. Another American squad is isolated at some distance from the battalion's main position, after 2nd Lt. Henry Herrick sees a scout, and runs after him, ordering his reluctant soldiers to follow. The scout lures them into an ambush, resulting in the majority of the platoon members' deaths, including Herrick's. Sgt. Savage assumes command of the squad, and by calling in artillery and using the cover of darkness, holds off the Vietnamese from their position.

The story switches between the Vietnamese and American points of view several times. Despite being trapped near the landing zone, and desperately outnumbered, the main force manages to hold off the Vietnamese with artillery, close air support, and even calling a last resort "Broken Arrow" at their most desperate point, killing some of their own soldiers but eliminating most of the Vietnamese offensive force. The American troopers regroup, secure the area and charge up the mountain where the Vietnamese division headquarters is located. The Vietnamese have set up heavy gun emplacements near the hidden entrance of the underground passage to the command post spoken of by the scout. Hal and his men charge right at them, into a seemingly impending massacre, but before the Vietnamese can fire, Major Bruce "Snakeshit" Crandall flies in with his helicopter and kills the Vietnamese guards with his side mounted machine guns.

Meanwhile, Nguyen Huu An the Vietnamese Commander is alerted that the Americans have broken through the lines, and the Base camp has no troops between command post and the Americans and the reserve forces were also without. He orders the headquarters evacuated. Later, Nguyen Huu An with some remaining soldiers collect the dead remains of his men The stranded platoon led by Savage are rescued. Moore, having completed his objective, returns to the L.Z. to be picked up, and, after all of his men, dead or alive, are removed from the battlefield, steps on to a helicopter and flies out of the valley. Strong visual emphasis is placed on Moore's being the last American to set foot off the field of battle. At the end of the movie it is revealed that the Landing Zone immediately reverted to North Vietnamese hands after the American troops helicoptered out. Hal Moore returned home safely after 235 more days of fighting.

Reception

The movie received mixed to fairly positive reviews. Roger Ebert from the *Chicago Sun-Times* gave the movie 3.5 stars out of 4 and praised the movie's battle scenes and how the movie follows the characters.

> *"Black Hawk Down" was criticized because the characters seemed hard to tell apart. "We Were Soldiers" doesn't have that problem; in the Hollywood tradition it identifies a few key players, casts them with stars, and follows their stories.*

Lisa Schwarzbaum from Entertainment Weekly gave the movie a B and noted the film's fair treatment of both sides.

> *"The writer-director bestows honor -- generously, apolitically -- not only on the dead and still living American veterans who fought in Ia Drang, but also on their families, on their Vietnamese adversaries, and on the families of their adversaries too. Rarely has a foe been portrayed with such measured respect for a separate reality, which should come as a relief to critics (I'm one) of the enemy's facelessness in* Black Hawk Down*; vignettes of gallantry among Vietnamese soldiers and such humanizing visual details as a Vietnamese sweetheart's photograph left behind in no way interfere with the primary, rousing saga of a fine American leader who kept his promise to his men to "leave no one behind dead or alive."*

David Sterritt from the *Christian Science Monitor* criticized the movie for giving a more positive image of the Vietnam War that didn't concur with reality.

> *"The films about Vietnam that most Americans remember are positively soaked in physical and emotional torment - from "Platoon," with its grunt's-eye view of combat, to "Apocalypse Now," with its exploration of war's dehumanizing insanity. Today, the pendulum has swung back again. If filmmakers with politically twisted knives once sliced away guts-and-glory clichés, their current equivalents hack away all meaningful concern with moral and political questions. We Were Soldiers" is shameless in this regard, filling the screen with square-jawed officers who weep at carnage and fresh-faced GIs who use their last breaths to intone things like, "I'm glad I died for my country."*

Todd McCarthy from Variety said the film *"presents the fighting realistically, violently and relatively coherently given the chaotic circumstances..."*. McCarthy further said *"Mel Gibson has the closest thing to a John Wayne part that anyone's played since the Duke himself rode into the sunset, and he plays it damn well."* He summarized with *"Gibson's performance anchors the film with commanding star power to burn. This officer truly loves his men, and the credibility with which the actor is able to express Moore's leadership qualities as well as his sensitive side is genuinely impressive."*

Hal Moore, who had long been critical of many Vietnam War films for their negative portrayals of American servicemen, publicly expressed approval of the film and is featured in segments of the DVD.

Some soldiers were less pleased: Retired Col Rick Rescorla, who plays an important role in the book, and whose photo is on the cover, was disappointed after reading the script to learn that he and his unit had been written out of the movie. In one key incident, the finding of a vintage French bugle on a dying Vietnamese soldier, Rescorla is replaced by a nameless *Welsh*—not Cornish—platoon leader.

Cast

- Mel Gibson - Lieutenant Colonel/Colonel Hal Moore
- Madeleine Stowe - Julia Moore
- Taylor Momsen - Julie Moore
- Luke Benward - David Moore
- Greg Kinnear - Major Bruce "Snakeshit" Crandall
- Sam Elliott - Sergeant Major Basil L. Plumley
- Chris Klein 2nd Lieutenant Jack Geoghegan
- Keri Russell - Barbara Geoghegan
- Barry Pepper - Joe Galloway
- Don Duong - Lieutenant Colonel Nguyen Huu An
- Ryan Hurst - Sergeant Ernie Savage
- Robert Bagnell - 1st Lieutenant Charlie Hastings
- Marc Blucas - 2nd Lieutenant Henry Herrick
- Josh Daugherty - Sp4. Robert Ouellette
- Jsu Garcia - Captain Tony Nadal
- Jon Hamm - Captain Matt Dillon
- Desmond Harrington - Sp4. Bill Beck
- Blake Heron - Sp4. Galen Bungum
- Clark Gregg - Captain Tom Metsker
- Erik MacArthur - Sp4. Russell Adams
- Dylan Walsh - Captain Robert Edwards
- Mark McCracken - Captain Ed "Too Tall" Freeman
- Edwin Morrow - Private First Class Willie Godboldt
- Brian Tee - Private First Class Jimmy Nakayama
- Sloane Momsen - Cecile Moore
- Bellamy Young - Catherine Metsker
- Simbi Khali - Alma Givens

See also

- Battle of Ia Drang
- *We Were Soldiers Once… And Young*
- Hal Moore
- Basil L. Plumley
- John Geoghegan
- 1st Cavalry Division
- Bruce Crandall
- Ed Freeman

External links

- *We Were Soldiers* [1] at the Internet Movie Database
- *We Were Soldiers* [2] at Box Office Mojo
- *We Were Soldiers* at [[Rotten Tomatoes|RottenTomatoes.com [3]]]

We Were Soldiers Once… And Young

We Were Soldiers Once… And Young

We Were Soldiers Once… And Young	
First edition title page	
Author	Lt. Gen. Harold G. Moore (Ret.) and Joseph L. Galloway
Country	United States of America
Language	English
Subject(s)	Vietnam, War
Genre(s)	Historical Non-fiction
Publisher	Random House
Publication date	October 20, 1992
Media type	Hardcover and Trade Paperback
Pages	432
ISBN	0679411585
OCLC Number	25832046 [1]
Dewey Decimal	959.704/342 20
LC Classification	DS557.8.I18 M66 1992

We Were Soldiers Once… And Young is a 1992 book, by Lt. Gen. Harold G. Moore (Ret.) and war journalist Joseph L. Galloway about the Vietnam War. It focuses on the role of the First and Second Battalions of the 7th Cavalry Regiment in the Battle of the Ia Drang Valley, the United States' first large-unit battle of the Vietnam War; previous engagements involved small units and patrols (squad, platoon, and company sized units).

Film adaptation

The book was adapted into the movie *We Were Soldiers*, directed by Randall Wallace and starring Mel Gibson as Moore. In the book, Moore complains that "Every damn Hollywood movie got it wrong"; Wallace has said he was inspired by this comment and became "determined to get it right this time."

The film's final version, though getting many of the facts of the book presented onto film, does not present an entirely historically accurate portrayal of the battle, nor is it entirely faithful to the book. For instance, the film depicts a heroic charge under the command of Lt. Col. Hal Moore at the end of the battle that destroys the Vietnamese reserve, ending the battle in an American victory (a fact that director Randall Wallace noted in the DVD commentary); in fact, there was no heroic final charge in the book, nor were the forces of the North Vietnamese destroyed, though, it should be noted, 1800 out 4000 Vietnamese soldiers were killed to 72, out of 395, American fatal casualties. Lt. Col. Nguyen Huu An, the Vietnamese commander, did not see the conclusion at LZ X-Ray as the end of combat, and the Battle of Ia Drang continued with combat action at LZ Albany where the 2/7th, with A Company 1/5th, found themselves in a fight for their lives against Lt Col Nguyen Huu An's reserve.

Finally, as the movie notes in a voice over by Joe Galloway (Barry Pepper), the battle continued for more than 300 more days.

There are as well many other historical differences in the book versus the movie; presumably to shorten the length of the movie. Some differences not shown would have demonstrated how desperate the American situation at Ia Drang was. For example, the seriousness of the overrun of C Company under the command of Capt Robert Edwards and the repulse of the final major North Vietnamese push at LZ X-Ray on the former C Company line which was then held by B Company 2/7th under the command of Capt Myron Diduryk, the Ukrainian Captain that Mel Gibson, as Col Moore, seems to claim is attached to the 1/7th. Also incorrect is the act of Capt. Ramon Nadal pushing forward and rescuing the stranded platoon of Lt. Henry Herrick, which according to the book was actually done not by one company of the 1/7th, but rather was a major push made by two companies of the 2/5th as well as B Company 1/7th.

Despite the aforementioned differences from the book and departures from historical accuracy, in a documentary included in the video versions, Gen. Moore states that this film is the first one "to get it right."

The Hanoi regime did not greet the film with approval. In fact, Don Duong the Vietnamese actor, who played the Vietnamese commander Lt. Col. Nguyen Huu An, was officially condemned as a traitor, subjected to interrogations to force him to sign a "confession" to "crimes" he had supposedly committed. Duong refused to give in. After months of negotiations between the Bush White House and Hanoi, Duong and his family were allowed to immigrate to the United States in 2003.

See also

- Hal Moore
- Joseph L. Galloway
- Battle of Ia Drang
- Mel Gibson
- Rick Rescorla

Book Editions

- ISBN 0679411585; Published: October 20, 1992, Random House Publishing Group, 432 pages (Hardcover)
- ISBN 0060013257; Published: April 15, 2002, Harper Perennial, 528 pages (Trade Paperback)
- ISBN 078624495X; Published: August 1, 2002, Thorndike Press, 688 pages (Hardcover)
- ISBN 0345472640; Published: June 29, 2004, Random House, 535 pages (Mass Market Paperbound)
- ISBN 034547581X; Published: November 23, 2004, Presidio Press, 432 pages (Trade Paperback)

External links

- Review by Andrew Ferguson [2]
- Website about the book with background information and links [3]
- Interview [3] with Joe Galloway and Hal Moore at the Pritzker Military Library
- Medal of Honor site - Major Bruce Crandall [6]

Joseph L. Galloway

Joseph Lee "Joe" Galloway (born November 13, 1941), is an American newspaper correspondent and columnist. He is the former Military Affairs consultant for the Knight-Ridder chain of newspapers and is presently a columnist with McClatchy Newspapers. During the Vietnam War, he often worked alongside the troops he covered and was awarded a Bronze Star for carrying wounded men to safety.

Personal life

Galloway is a native of Refugio, Texas. His first wife Theresa M. Galloway (May 12, 1948-January 26, 1996) died of cancer. They had two sons, Joshua and Lee. In 1998, Galloway married Karen Metsker, daughter of Capt. Tom Metsker, a battalion intelligence officer killed in the Vietnam War. Galloway now resides in his home county of Refugio County, Texas in Bayside in a cottage overlooking Copano Bay.

Career

Newspapers

Galloway started his career at the *Victoria Advocate* in Texas, afterwards working for United Press International (UPI) in the Kansas City and Topeka bureaus. Later, he served overseas as bureau chief or regional manager in Tokyo, Vietnam, Jakarta, New Delhi, Singapore, Moscow, and Los Angeles.

During the Vietnam War, Galloway served three tours for UPI, beginning in early 1965. Decorated for rescuing wounded American soldiers under heavy enemy fire during the battle at Landing Zone X-Ray in the Ia Drang Valley, he was the only civilian awarded the Bronze Star by the United States Army during that war.

Literature

Along with Lt. Gen. Harold G. Moore, Galloway co-authored a detailed account of those experiences in the best-selling 1992 book, *We Were Soldiers Once ... And Young*. A sequel was released in 2008: *We Are Soldiers Still: A Journey Back to the Battlefields of Vietnam*.

In Popular Culture

In *We Were Soldiers*, a 2002 film based on his 1992 book, Galloway is portrayed by actor Barry Pepper.

Narration

Galloway narrated *A Flag Between Two Families*, a documentary film based on the events of May 9, 1968 in Vietnam by the members of Charlie Company, 1st Battalion, 5th Cavalry.

Awards

In 1991, Galloway received a National Magazine Award for a *U.S. News* cover article on the Ia Drang battles in Vietnam.In 1992 he received the New Media Award of the National VFW for his coverage of the Persian Gulf War for U.S. News. In 2002 Galloway received the Robert Denig Award for Exceptional Service of the U.S. Marine Corps Combat Correspondents Assn. In 2006 he received the Tex McCrary Award of the Congressional Medal of Honor Society.

In 1998, Galloway received a Bronze Star with Valor "V" device for rescuing wounded soldiers under fire in the Battle of Ia Drang in Vietnam in November 1965. His was the only medal awarded to a civilian by the U.S. Army for valor during the Vietnam War.

Commentaries

George W. Bush administration

In a number of columns, Galloway has spoken out against the Iraq War and George W. Bush. In a column on July 6, 2007, Galloway asked why the Bush administration "looks remarkably more like an organized crime ring than one of the arms of the American government?" He further asks what happened to the George W. Bush he voted for in 2000 and who promised to give a government "whose appointees would be honest, upright, fair and moral." On March 13, 2008 he published a commentary titled "When Will It End?" that asked, "[t]he next time that we Americans start thinking about maybe electing someone with no known talent, limited useful experience and an IQ that's barely equal to his body temperature, what say we just leave the presidency vacant and the White House shuttered for eight years or so?"

External links

- Joseph L. Galloway columns on the McClatchy website [1]
- Interview [3] on *We Were Soldiers Once ... And Young* at the Pritzker Military Library
- Interview [2] on *We Are Soldiers Still*

Bruce P. Crandall

Bruce P. Crandall

Bruce Perry Crandall	
Born 1933 (age 77–78)	
 Major Bruce P. Crandall (1965), Medal of Honor recipient	
Place of birth	Olympia, Washington
Allegiance	United States of America
Service/branch	United States Army
Years of service	1953-1977
Rank	Lieutenant Colonel
Battles/wars	**Vietnam War** *Battle of Ia Drang
Awards	Medal of Honor Distinguished Service Cross Distinguished Flying Cross (4) Bronze Star Purple Heart
Other work	City Manager, Dunsmuir, California Public Works Manager, Mesa, Arizona

Bruce P. Crandall (born 1933) is a retired U.S. Army officer who received the Medal of Honor for his actions during the Battle of Ia Drang. During the battle he flew 22 missions in an unarmed helicopter into enemy fire to bring ammunition and supplies and evacuate the wounded. By the end of the Vietnam War, he had flown over 900 combat missions.

After retiring from the Army he worked several jobs in different states before settling down with his wife in his home state of Washington.

Early life and family

Crandall was born in 1933 and raised in Olympia, Washington and during high school became an All-American baseball player. After graduating he attended the University of Washington in Seattle until being drafted into the U.S. Army in 1953. He married his wife Arlene on March 31, 1956 and they have three sons and five grandchildren. They currently reside in Washington state.

Military service

After commissioning and graduation from fixed-wing and helicopter training conducted by the United States Air Force and United States Army, he was assigned to an Army Aviation mapping group based out of the Presidio of San Francisco *"that at the time was the largest flying military aviation unit in the world"*. From there he went on to fly Cessna L-19 Bird Dogs and de Havilland Canada DHC-2 Beavers in Alaska, again for topographic studies. His first overseas flying assignment was to Wheelus Air Base in Tripoli, Libya, mapping the desert for two years flying de Havilland Canada DHC-3 Otter, Beaver, Birddog and OH-23 Raven aircraft as an instructor pilot and unit test pilot.

His next overseas tours were flying over thousands of square miles of previously unmapped mountains and jungles in Central and South America. For this mission, he was based out of Howard Air Force Base, Panama, and Costa Rica. While assigned to the 11th Air Assault Division, Crandall helped develop air-assault tactics as a platoon commander. In early 1965, he joined the Dominican Republic Expeditionary Force as a liaison to the 18th Airborne Corps. Later that year, he would command the 1st Cavalry Division's Company A, 229th Assault Helicopter Battalion at An Khe, Vietnam. Using the call sign "Ancient Serpent 6", he led a flying unit supporting eight battalions on the ground.

On November 14, 1965, he led the first major division operation of air mobile troops into Landing Zone X-Ray in Vietnam's Battle of Ia Drang and is credited with evacuating some 70 wounded comrades with his wing man and fellow Medal of Honor recipient Major Ed Freeman. The two also flew in the ammunition needed for the 7th Cavalry to survive. The craft he was flying was unarmed. On February 26, 2007, Crandall received the Medal of Honor from President George W. Bush in a ceremony in the East Room of the White House for his actions on November 14.

In January 1966, during the first combined American and South Vietnamese Army operation, "Operation Masher", Crandall, while under intense enemy fire and with only a spot flashlight beam to guide him, twice dropped his Huey helicopter through the dense jungle canopy to rescue 12 wounded soldiers. For his courage in that incident Crandall received the Aviation & Space Writers Helicopter Heroism Award for 1966.

After an assignment in Colorado, he attended the Armed Forces Staff College. Soon he was back in Vietnam, this time flying Huey gunships - *"a big improvement"* -- supporting the 1st Battalion, 9th Cavalry Squadron, 1st Cavalry Division.

In January 1968, four months into his second tour, Crandall's helicopter was downed during another rescue attempt due to Air Force bombs going off too close to where he was flying. After five months in the hospital, with a broken back and other injuries, he resumed his career as a student earning a bootstrap degree through the University of Nebraska in 1969. In Bangkok, Thailand, he would become a facility engineer managing 3800 people. He subsequently served as deputy chief of staff, deputy installation commander, and commander of the 5th Engineer Combat Battalion, all at Fort Leonard Wood in Missouri.

South America was supposed to be his next assignment, and he and his wife, Arlene, attended the Defense Language Institute, Monterey, California, as Spanish language students in preparation as aviation and engineering adviser to Argentina, an assignment which never came. A stroke sidelined Crandall, ending his flying career. After his recovery, the Crandalls did find the language training useful when he was sent to Caracas, Venezuela, as the Defense Mapping Agency's director for the Inter-American Geodetic Survey.

In his final Army assignment, he served as senior engineer adviser to the California Army National Guard and then in 1977 he retired from the Army as a lieutenant colonel.

Later life

After retiring from the Army he received a Master's Degree in Public Administration from Golden Gate University in 1977. Since retiring he has held several different jobs including spending three years as the city manager of Dunsmuir, California. After leaving California he and his wife moved to Mesa, Arizona where he spent 17 years working in the Public Works Department, the last four as the public works manager.

Honors and awards

Crandall has received the following military decorations.

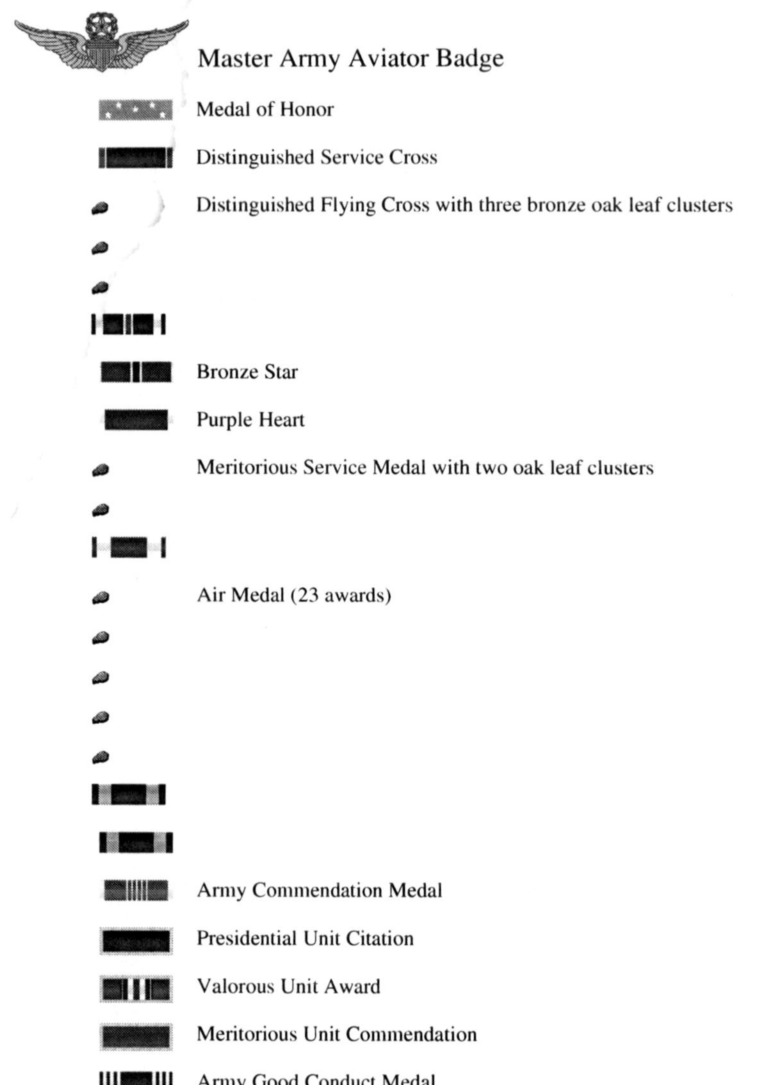

Master Army Aviator Badge

Medal of Honor

Distinguished Service Cross

Distinguished Flying Cross with three bronze oak leaf clusters

Bronze Star

Purple Heart

Meritorious Service Medal with two oak leaf clusters

Air Medal (23 awards)

Army Commendation Medal

Presidential Unit Citation

Valorous Unit Award

Meritorious Unit Commendation

Army Good Conduct Medal

National Defense Service Medal with one bronze oak leaf cluster

Armed Forces Expeditionary Medal

Vietnam Service Medal with three bronze service stars

Armed Forces Reserve Medal

Vietnam Cross of Gallantry with Palm and Gold Star (only highest device is worn)

Vietnam Gallantry Cross Unit Citation with Palm (Awarded per Army General Order 8) *(not worn)*

Vietnam Campaign Medal

Medal of Honor citation

For conspicuous gallantry and intrepidity at the risk of his life above and beyond the call of duty: Major Bruce P. Crandall distinguished himself by extraordinary heroism as a Flight Commander in the Republic of Vietnam, while serving with Company A, 229th Assault Helicopter Battalion, 1st Cavalry Division (Airmobile). On 14 November 1965, his flight of sixteen helicopters was lifting troops for a search and destroy mission from Plei Me, Vietnam, to Landing Zone X-Ray in the Ia Drang Valley. On the fourth troop lift, the airlift began to take enemy fire, and by the time the aircraft had refueled and returned for the next troop lift, the enemy had Landing Zone X-Ray targeted. As Major Crandall and the first eight helicopters landed to discharge troops on his fifth troop lift, his unarmed helicopter came under such intense enemy fire that the ground commander ordered the second flight of eight aircraft to abort their mission. As Major Crandall flew back to Plei Me, his base of operations, he determined that the ground commander of the besieged infantry battalion desperately needed more ammunition. Major Crandall then decided to adjust his base of operations to Artillery Firebase Falcon in order to shorten the flight distance to deliver ammunition and evacuate wounded soldiers. While medical evacuation was not his mission, he immediately sought volunteers and with complete disregard for his own personal safety, led the two aircraft to Landing Zone X-Ray. Despite the fact that the landing zone was still under relentless enemy fire, Major Crandall landed and proceeded to supervise the loading of seriously wounded soldiers aboard his aircraft. Major Crandall's voluntary decision to land under the most extreme fire instilled in the other pilots the will and spirit to continue to land their own aircraft, and in the ground forces the realization that they would be resupplied and that friendly wounded

Bruce Crandall receiving the Medal of Honor

would be promptly evacuated. This greatly enhanced morale and the will to fight at a critical time. After his first medical evacuation, Major Crandall continued to fly into and out of the landing zone throughout the day and into the evening. That day he completed a total of 22 flights, most under intense enemy fire, retiring from the battlefield only after all possible service had been rendered to the Infantry battalion. His actions provided critical resupply of ammunition and evacuation of the wounded. Major Crandall's daring acts of bravery and courage in the face of an overwhelming and determined enemy are in keeping with the highest traditions of the military service and reflect great credit upon himself, his unit, and the United States Army.

Other honors

He has been inducted into the United States Air Force's "Gathering of Eagles" in 1994 and the Army Aviation Hall of Fame in 2004.

In 2001, Crandall was an aviation consultant on the 2002 movie *We Were Soldiers* about the Battle of Ia Drang. Crandall was portrayed in the film by Greg Kinnear.

The Olympia High School Baseball Field was named after Lt. Col. Crandall in a ceremony prior to the 2007 season. Crandall was a High School All-American baseball player for Olympia High School.

See also

- List of Medal of Honor recipients for the Vietnam War
- List of University of Washington people
- List of Golden Gate University people

References

This article incorporates text in the public domain from the United States Army.

- "Bruce P.Crandall - Medal of Honor, U.S. Army" [1]. U.S. Army, army.mil. Retrieved February 15, 2010.
- Gomez, Ian (February 22, 2007). "Vietnam pilot to receive Medal of Honor" [2]. *USA Today*.
- Office of the Press Secretary (February 26, 2007). "President Bush Presents the Medal of Honor to Lieutenant Colonel Bruce Crandall" [3]. *www.whitehouse.gov*.

External links

- "Bruce P. Crandall" [4]. *Hall of Valor*. Military Times. Retrieved February 15, 2010.
- "Interview with Bruce P Crandall" [5]. Pritzker Military Library. April 22, 2008. Retrieved February 15, 2010.

Ed Freeman

Ed Freeman

Ed W. Freeman	
November 20, 1927 – August 20, 2008 (aged 80)	
  Ed Freeman (left) is congratulated by President George W. Bush after receiving his award.	
Nickname	Too Tall
Place of birth	Neely, Mississippi
Place of death	Boise, Idaho
Resting place	Idaho State Veterans Cemetery, Boise, Idaho
Allegiance	United States of America
Service/branch	United States Navy United States Army
Years of service	1944 - 1946 (Navy) 1946 - 1967 (Army)
Rank	Major
Unit	229th Assault Helicopter Battalion, 1st Cavalry Division (Airmobile)
Battles/wars	World War II Korean War • Battle of Pork Chop Hill Vietnam War • Battle of Ia Drang
Awards	Medal of Honor

Ed W. "Too Tall" Freeman (November 20, 1927 - August 20, 2008) was a United States Army helicopter pilot who received the U.S. military's highest decoration, the Medal of Honor, for his actions in the Battle of Ia Drang during the Vietnam War. During the battle, he flew through gunfire numerous times, bringing supplies to a trapped American battalion and flying dozens of wounded soldiers to safety. Freeman was a wing-man for Major Bruce Crandall who also received the Medal of Honor for the same missions.

Early life

Freeman was born in Neely, Greene County, Mississippi, the sixth of nine children. When he was 13 years old, he saw thousands of men on maneuvers pass by his home in Mississippi. He knew then that he would become a soldier.

He grew up in nearby McLain and graduated from Washington High School. At age 17, before graduating from high school, Ed enlisted in the U.S. Navy and served on the USS *Cacapon* (AO-52) for two years. Once the war was over, he returned to his hometown and graduated high school. Immediately afterwards, he joined the Army. On April 30, 1954, he married Barbara Morgan. They had two sons, Mike, born in 1956 and Doug, born in 1962.

Military service

Beyond his service in the Navy in World War II, he reached the Army rank of first sergeant by the time of the Korean War. Although he was in the Corps of Engineers, he fought as an infantry soldier in Korea. He participated in the Battle of Pork Chop Hill and earned a battlefield commission as one of only 14 survivors out of 257 men who made it through the opening stages of the battle. His second lieutenant-bars were pinned on by General James Van Fleet personally. The commission made him eligible to become a pilot, a childhood dream of his. He then assumed command of B Company and led them back up Pork Chop Hill. However, when he applied for pilot training he was told that, at six feet four inches, he was "too tall" for pilot duty. The phrase stuck, and he was known by the nickname of "Too Tall" for the rest of his career.

In 1955, the height limit for pilots was raised and Freeman was accepted into flying school. He first flew airplanes before switching to helicopters. After the Korean War, he flew the world on mapping missions. By the time he was sent to Vietnam in 1965, he was an experienced helicopter pilot and was placed second-in-command of his sixteen-craft unit. He served as a captain in Company A, 229th Assault Helicopter Battalion, 1st Cavalry Division (Airmobile).

Vietnam service

On November 14, 1965, Freeman and his unit transported a battalion of American soldiers to the Ia Drang Valley. Later, after arriving back at base, they learned that the soldiers had come under intense fire and had taken heavy casualties. Enemy fire around the landing zones was so heavy that the medical evacuation helicopters refused to fly in to the landing zone. Freeman and his commander, Major Bruce

Crandall, volunteered to fly their unarmed, lightly armored UH-I Huey in support of the embattled troops. Freeman made a total of fourteen trips to the battlefield, bringing in water and ammunition and taking out wounded soldiers from what was later named the Battle of Ia Drang. By the time they grounded their wounded huey, Capt. Freeman had been wounded four times by ground fire.

Retirement

Freeman was sent home from Vietnam in 1966 and retired from the military the next year. He settled in the Treasure Valley area of Idaho, his wife Barbara's home state, and continued to work as a pilot. He flew helicopters for another 20 years, fighting wildfires, conducting animal censuses, and herding wild horses for the Department of the Interior until his second retirement in 1991. By then, he had 17,000 flight hours in helicopters and 8,000 in fixed-wing aircraft.

Medal of Honor nomination

Main article: Battle of Ia Drang

Freeman's commanding officer nominated him for the Medal of Honor for his actions at Ia Drang, but not in time to meet a two-year deadline then in place. He was instead awarded the Distinguished Flying Cross. The Medal of Honor nomination was disregarded until 1995, when the two-year deadline was removed. He was formally presented with the medal on July 16, 2001, in the East Room of the White House by President George W. Bush.

Medal of Honor citation

Freeman's official Medal of Honor citation reads:

Army version of the Medal of Honor

> "Captain Ed W. Freeman, United States Army, distinguished himself by numerous acts of conspicuous gallantry and extraordinary intrepidity on 14 November 1965 while serving with Company A, 229th Assault Helicopter Battalion, 1st Cavalry Division (Airmobile). As a flight leader and second in command of a 16-helicopter lift unit, he supported a heavily engaged American infantry battalion at Landing Zone X-Ray in the Ia Drang Valley, Republic of Vietnam. The unit was almost out of ammunition after taking some of the heaviest casualties of the war, fighting off a relentless attack from a highly motivated, heavily armed enemy force. When the infantry commander closed the helicopter landing zone due to intense direct enemy fire, Captain Freeman risked his own life by flying his unarmed helicopter through a gauntlet of enemy fire time after time, delivering critically needed ammunition, water and medical supplies to the besieged battalion. His flights had a direct impact on the battle's outcome by providing the engaged units with timely supplies of ammunition critical to their survival, without which they would almost surely have gone down, with much greater loss of life. After medical evacuation helicopters refused to fly into the area due to intense enemy fire, Captain Freeman flew 14 separate rescue missions, providing life-saving evacuation of an estimated 30 seriously wounded soldiers -- some of whom would not have survived had he not acted. All flights were made into a small emergency landing zone within 100 to 200 meters of the defensive perimeter where heavily committed units were perilously holding off the attacking elements. Captain Freeman's selfless acts of great valor, extraordinary perseverance and intrepidity were far above and beyond the call of duty or mission and set a superb example of leadership and courage for all of his peers. Captain Freeman's extraordinary heroism and devotion to duty are in keeping with the highest traditions of military service and reflect great credit upon himself, his unit and the United States Army."

Military awards

His awards include:

- Medal of Honor
- Distinguished Flying Cross

Death and legacy

Freeman died on August 20, 2008 due to complications from Parkinson's disease. He was buried with full military honors at the Idaho State Veterans Cemetery in Boise.

In the 2002 film *We Were Soldiers*, which depicted the Battle of Ia Drang, Freeman was portrayed by Mark McCracken. The post office in Freeman's hometown of McLain, Mississippi, was renamed the "Major Ed W. Freeman Post Office" in March 2009.

See also

- List of Medal of Honor recipients for the Vietnam War

References

This article incorporates public domain material from websites or documents of the United States Army Center of Military History.

External links

- "Ed W. Freeman" [1]. *Claim to Fame: Medal of Honor recipients*. Find a Grave. Retrieved September 2, 2010.

Julia Compton Moore

Julia Compton Moore

Julia Compton Moore	
Born	February 10, 1929 Fort Sill, OK
Died	April 18, 2004 (aged 75) Auburn, Alabama
Occupation	Army daughter, wife, and mother
Spouse	Hal Moore

Julia Compton Moore (February 10, 1929 - April 18, 2004) was a U.S. Army daughter, wife, and mother, who was depicted in the film *We Were Soldiers* by actress Madeleine Stowe. Her efforts and complaints in the aftermath of the Battle of Ia Drang prompted the Army to set up survivor support networks and casualty notification teams consisting of uniformed officers, which are still in use.

Biography

Julia Compton was born in Fort Sill, Oklahoma, the only child of Army Colonel Louis J. Compton and Elizabeth Boon Compton. From the age of 12, she began a lifelong journey of experiencing the separation and risk of loss in war. Her father fought in Europe in World War II, her husband was wounded in Korea and Vietnam, and one of her sons fought with the 82nd Airborne Division in Panama and the Gulf War.

Education

Compton was a graduate of Chevy Chase Junior College, Chevy Chase, Maryland and attended the University of North Carolina at Chapel Hill, as a member of Pi Beta Phi Sorority, prior to her marriage.

Marriage and children

Julia Compton was married in 1949 to Hal Moore, who later commanded the 1st Battalion, 7th Cavalry in the battle of the Ia Drang Valley in Vietnam in 1965. They have five children:

- Greg Moore

- LTC Steve Moore, USA (Ret)
- Julie Moore Orlowski
- Cecile Moore Rainey
- COL David Moore, USA

Contributions to Army family life

Wherever her husband was stationed, Mrs. Moore served as a Brownie and Girl Scout Leader and Cub Scout Den Mother. She volunteered with the Red Cross in the Army hospitals. She supported the day care centers and worked with the wives clubs to take better care of the enlisted soldier and his family. Mrs. Moore was especially active in setting up the Army Community Service organizations that are now a permanent fixture on all army posts and which assist each soldier as they process into their new duty stations.

Casualty notification

The Ia Drang Campaign was the first major ground engagement involving U.S forces in Vietnam. The Army had not yet set up an adequate system of notifying the next of kin of battlefield fatalities. Instead, the telegrams were given to taxi cab drivers for delivery, as depicted in the film *We Were Soldiers*. Unlike the film depiction, Mrs. Moore did not actually assume responsibility for the delivery of the telegrams, but followed in the wake of the taxis, grieving with widows and families, and attending the funerals of those who fell under her husband's command. Her complaints to the Pentagon, and the example that she set, prompted the Army to immediately set up notification teams consisting of a uniformed officer and a chaplain.

Burial

Mrs. Moore is buried at the Fort Benning Cemetery, near her mother and father, and in the middle of the 7th Cavalry troopers, beside the grave of SGT Jack E. Gell of Alpha Company, 1st Battalion, 7th Cavalry.

Julia Compton Moore Award

One of Julia Moore's more important contributions to the quality of Army family life is summed up by the Ben Franklin Global Forum's press release, announcing the establishment of the Julia Compton Moore Award:

> “Mrs. Moore's actions to change Pentagon death notification policy in the aftermath of the historic battle of the Ia Drang Valley represents a significant contribution to our nation. Prior to Mrs. Moore's intervention, Pentagon policy was to notify families by a telegram delivered by cab drivers. It serves today as a shining example of one of Mrs. Moore's many contributions to the morale and welfare of the Army family.”

The award recognizes the civilian spouses of soldiers for "Outstanding Contributions to the United States Army".

See also

- Battle of Ia Drang
- We Were Soldiers
- We Were Soldiers Once ... And Young
- Joseph L. Galloway
- Hal Moore

References

- Moore, Hal; Joseph L. Galloway (2004). *We Were Soldiers Once ... And Young*. Random House. pp. 535. ISBN 0345472640.

Article Sources and Contributors

Hal Moore *Source*: http://en.wikipedia.org/?oldid=390455935 *Contributors*: 1 anonymous edits

Battle of Ia Drang *Source*: http://en.wikipedia.org/?oldid=390546858 *Contributors*: Nirvana77

We Were Soldiers *Source*: http://en.wikipedia.org/?oldid=388128581 *Contributors*:

We Were Soldiers Once… And Young *Source*: http://en.wikipedia.org/?oldid=389384852 *Contributors*: R'n'B

Joseph L. Galloway *Source*: http://en.wikipedia.org/?oldid=384934832 *Contributors*: Umrguy42

Bruce P. Crandall *Source*: http://en.wikipedia.org/?oldid=389602750 *Contributors*:

Ed Freeman *Source*: http://en.wikipedia.org/?oldid=389236558 *Contributors*: Kumioko

Julia Compton Moore *Source*: http://en.wikipedia.org/?oldid=390424480 *Contributors*: Kumioko

Image Sources, Licenses and Contributors

Image:LTG(R) Hal Moore at West Point 10 May 2010.JPG *Source*: http://en.wikipedia.org/w/index.php?title=File:LTG(R)_Hal_Moore_at_West_Point_10_May_2010.JPG *License*: Creative Commons Attribution-Sharealike 3.0 *Contributors*: User:Ahodges7

File:Flag of the United States.svg *Source*: http://en.wikipedia.org/w/index.php?title=File:Flag_of_the_United_States.svg *License*: Public Domain *Contributors*: User:Dbenbenn, User:Indolences, User:Jacobolus, User:Technion, User:Zscout370

File:United States Department of the Army Seal.svg *Source*: http://en.wikipedia.org/w/index.php?title=File:United_States_Department_of_the_Army_Seal.svg *License*: Public Domain *Contributors*: U.S. Dept. of Defense

File:CIB2.gif *Source*: http://en.wikipedia.org/w/index.php?title=File:CIB2.gif *License*: Public Domain *Contributors*: US Air Force

File:ArmyAvnBadge.gif *Source*: http://en.wikipedia.org/w/index.php?title=File:ArmyAvnBadge.gif *License*: Public Domain *Contributors*: Beao, CORNELIUSSEON, FieldMarine, Iamdavidtheking, Kintetsubuffalo, Perhelion

File:OldAirmobileBadge.gif *Source*: http://en.wikipedia.org/w/index.php?title=File:OldAirmobileBadge.gif *License*: Public Domain *Contributors*: Original uploader was Mamettler at en.wikipedia

File:SecDefBadge.gif *Source*: http://en.wikipedia.org/w/index.php?title=File:SecDefBadge.gif *License*: Public Domain *Contributors*: FieldMarine, Iamdavidtheking, SGT141

File:GeneralStaffID.gif *Source*: http://en.wikipedia.org/w/index.php?title=File:GeneralStaffID.gif *License*: Public Domain *Contributors*: CORNELIUSSEON, Clindberg, FieldMarine, Foroa, Iamdavidtheking, Joey-das-WBF, Koavf, SGT141

File:1st Cavalry Division - Shoulder Sleeve Insignia.svg *Source*: http://en.wikipedia.org/w/index.php?title=File:1st_Cavalry_Division_-_Shoulder_Sleeve_Insignia.svg *License*: Public Domain *Contributors*: Avron, Beria, CORNELIUSSEON, FieldMarine, Mandavi, 1 anonymous edits

File:7thCav.JPG *Source*: http://en.wikipedia.org/w/index.php?title=File:7thCav.JPG *License*: Public Domain *Contributors*: User:Jrcrin001

File:Distinguished Service Cross ribbon.svg *Source*: http://en.wikipedia.org/w/index.php?title=File:Distinguished_Service_Cross_ribbon.svg *License*: Public Domain *Contributors*: user:Ipankonin

Image:Distinguished Service Medal ribbon.svg *Source*: http://en.wikipedia.org/w/index.php?title=File:Distinguished_Service_Medal_ribbon.svg *License*: Public Domain *Contributors*: user:Ipankonin

Image:Bronze oakleaf-3d.svg *Source*: http://en.wikipedia.org/w/index.php?title=File:Bronze_oakleaf-3d.svg *License*: Public Domain *Contributors*: lestatdelc

Image:Legion of Merit ribbon.svg *Source*: http://en.wikipedia.org/w/index.php?title=File:Legion_of_Merit_ribbon.svg *License*: Public Domain *Contributors*: user:Ipankonin

Image:Valor device.svg *Source*: http://en.wikipedia.org/w/index.php?title=File:Valor_device.svg *License*: Public Domain *Contributors*: user:Ipankonin

Image:Bronze Star ribbon.svg *Source*: http://en.wikipedia.org/w/index.php?title=File:Bronze_Star_ribbon.svg *License*: Public Domain *Contributors*: user:Ipankonin

Image:Silver oakleaf-3d.svg *Source*: http://en.wikipedia.org/w/index.php?title=File:Silver_oakleaf-3d.svg *License*: Public Domain *Contributors*: User:Lestatdelc

Image:Air Medal ribbon.svg *Source*: http://en.wikipedia.org/w/index.php?title=File:Air_Medal_ribbon.svg *License*: Public Domain *Contributors*: user:Ipankonin

Image:Joint Service Commendation ribbon.svg *Source*: http://en.wikipedia.org/w/index.php?title=File:Joint_Service_Commendation_ribbon.svg *License*: Public Domain *Contributors*: user:Ipankonin

Image:Army Commendation Medal ribbon.svg *Source*: http://en.wikipedia.org/w/index.php?title=File:Army_Commendation_Medal_ribbon.svg *License*: Public Domain *Contributors*: US Army

Image:Presidential Unit Citation ribbon.svg *Source*: http://en.wikipedia.org/w/index.php?title=File:Presidential_Unit_Citation_ribbon.svg *License*: Public Domain *Contributors*: user:Ipankonin

Image:American Campaign Medal ribbon.svg *Source*: http://en.wikipedia.org/w/index.php?title=File:American_Campaign_Medal_ribbon.svg *License*: Public Domain *Contributors*: user:Ipankonin

Image:Asiatic-Pacific Campaign ribbon.svg *Source*: http://en.wikipedia.org/w/index.php?title=File:Asiatic-Pacific_Campaign_ribbon.svg *License*: Public Domain *Contributors*: user:Ipankonin

Image:World War II Victory Medal ribbon.svg *Source*: http://en.wikipedia.org/w/index.php?title=File:World_War_II_Victory_Medal_ribbon.svg *License*: Public Domain *Contributors*: user:Ipankonin

Image:Army of Occupation ribbon.svg *Source*: http://en.wikipedia.org/w/index.php?title=File:Army_of_Occupation_ribbon.svg *License*: Public Domain *Contributors*: user:Ipankonin

Image:National Defense Service Medal ribbon.svg *Source*: http://en.wikipedia.org/w/index.php?title=File:National_Defense_Service_Medal_ribbon.svg *License*: Public Domain *Contributors*: user:Ipankonin

Image:Bronze-service-star-3d.png *Source*: http://en.wikipedia.org/w/index.php?title=File:Bronze-service-star-3d.png *License*: Creative Commons Attribution-Sharealike 3.0 *Contributors*: User:Lestatdelc

Image:KSMRib.svg *Source*: http://en.wikipedia.org/w/index.php?title=File:KSMRib.svg *License*: Public Domain *Contributors*: user:Ipankonin

Image:Vietnam Service Ribbon.svg *Source*: http://en.wikipedia.org/w/index.php?title=File:Vietnam_Service_Ribbon.svg *License*: Public Domain *Contributors*: user:Ipankonin

Image:AFEMRib.svg *Source*: http://en.wikipedia.org/w/index.php?title=File:AFEMRib.svg *License*: GNU Free Documentation License *Contributors*: user:Shazz

Image:Vietnam gallantry cross-w-palm-3d.svg *Source*: http://en.wikipedia.org/w/index.php?title=File:Vietnam_gallantry_cross-w-palm-3d.svg *License*: Creative Commons Attribution-Sharealike 3.0 *Contributors*: User:Lestatdelc

Image:Presidential Unit Citation (Korea).svg *Source*: http://en.wikipedia.org/w/index.php?title=File:Presidential_Unit_Citation_(Korea).svg *License*: Public Domain *Contributors*: User:Inductiveload

File:Vietnam gallantry cross unit award-3d.svg *Source*: http://en.wikipedia.org/w/index.php?title=File:Vietnam_gallantry_cross_unit_award-3d.svg *License*: Creative Commons Attribution-Sharealike 3.0 *Contributors*: User:Lestatdelc

Image:United Nations Service Medal for Korea ribbon.png *Source*: http://en.wikipedia.org/w/index.php?title=File:United_Nations_Service_Medal_for_Korea_ribbon.png *License*: Public Domain *Contributors*: Original uploader was

PalawanOz at en.wikipedia

Image:Vietnam Campaign Medal ribbon.png *Source*: http://en.wikipedia.org/w/index.php?title=File:Vietnam_Campaign_Medal_ribbon.png *License*: Public Domain *Contributors*: Original uploader was PalawanOz at en.wikipedia

Image:Korean War Service Medal ribbon.png *Source*: http://en.wikipedia.org/w/index.php?title=File:Korean_War_Service_Medal_ribbon.png *License*: Public Domain *Contributors*: User:PalawanOz

File:Flag of North Vietnam.svg *Source*: http://en.wikipedia.org/w/index.php?title=File:Flag_of_North_Vietnam.svg *License*: Public Domain *Contributors*: Anime Addict AA, Antemister, Fry1989, Gabbe, Homo lupus, Madden, Nilfanion, Officer781, R-41, Zscout370, Владимир турчанинов, 1 anonymous edits

Image:FNL Flag.svg *Source*: http://en.wikipedia.org/w/index.php?title=File:FNL_Flag.svg *License*: Public Domain *Contributors*: Anime Addict AA, Denelson83, Homo lupus, MS05L, Madden, Masturbius, Mattes, Mikrobølgeovn, Mister C4, Mnmazur, Mogelzahn, R-41, Thisisbossi, 10 anonymous edits

File:Flag of South Vietnam.svg *Source*: http://en.wikipedia.org/w/index.php?title=File:Flag_of_South_Vietnam.svg *License*: Public Domain *Contributors*: Anime Addict AA, Antemister, Avia, ChongDae, Conscious, Editor at Large, Electron, Fry1989, Gryffindor, Homo lupus, Kauffner, Ludger1961, MS05L, Madden, Mattes, Multichill, ThomasPusch, Thorjoetunheim, Zscout370, 22 anonymous edits

File:Ia Drang Infantry disembarking from Helicopter.jpg *Source*: http://en.wikipedia.org/w/index.php?title=File:Ia_Drang_Infantry_disembarking_from_Helicopter.jpg *License*: Public Domain *Contributors*: US Army

File:Ia Drang X-ray perimeter situation 14. november.jpg *Source*: http://en.wikipedia.org/w/index.php?title=File:Ia_Drang_X-ray_perimeter_situation_14._november.jpg *License*: Public Domain *Contributors*: User:Gunfighter-6

File:Ia Drang X-ray relief 15. november.jpg *Source*: http://en.wikipedia.org/w/index.php?title=File:Ia_Drang_X-ray_relief_15._november.jpg *License*: Public Domain *Contributors*: User:Gunfighter-6

File:BruceCrandall.jpg *Source*: http://en.wikipedia.org/w/index.php?title=File:BruceCrandall.jpg *License*: Public Domain *Contributors*: w:United States Army photo

File:cmoh army.jpg *Source*: http://en.wikipedia.org/w/index.php?title=File:Cmoh_army.jpg *License*: Public Domain *Contributors*: Amire80, Jwillbur

File:US Army Master Aviator Badge.png *Source*: http://en.wikipedia.org/w/index.php?title=File:US_Army_Master_Aviator_Badge.png *License*: Public Domain *Contributors*: CORNELIUSSEON, Darz Mol, FieldMarine

File:Medal of Honor ribbon.svg *Source*: http://en.wikipedia.org/w/index.php?title=File:Medal_of_Honor_ribbon.svg *License*: Public Domain *Contributors*: user:Ipankonin

Image:Distinguished Flying Cross ribbon.svg *Source*: http://en.wikipedia.org/w/index.php?title=File:Distinguished_Flying_Cross_ribbon.svg *License*: Public Domain *Contributors*: user:Ipankonin

File:Purple Heart BAR.svg *Source*: http://en.wikipedia.org/w/index.php?title=File:Purple_Heart_BAR.svg *License*: Public Domain *Contributors*: Alno, Arch dude, CORNELIUSSEON, Ipankonin, Jappalang, Jatkins, Juiced lemon, Madmedea, Mboro, Orem

Image:Meritorious Service ribbon.svg *Source*: http://en.wikipedia.org/w/index.php?title=File:Meritorious_Service_ribbon.svg *License*: Public Domain *Contributors*: user:Ipankonin

File:Air Medal ribbon.svg *Source*: http://en.wikipedia.org/w/index.php?title=File:Air_Medal_ribbon.svg *License*: Public Domain *Contributors*: user:Ipankonin

File:Army Commendation Medal ribbon.svg *Source*: http://en.wikipedia.org/w/index.php?title=File:Army_Commendation_Medal_ribbon.svg *License*: Public Domain *Contributors*: US Army

File:Presidential Unit Citation ribbon.svg *Source*: http://en.wikipedia.org/w/index.php?title=File:Presidential_Unit_Citation_ribbon.svg *License*: Public Domain *Contributors*: user:Ipankonin

File:Valorous Unit Award ribbon.svg *Source*: http://en.wikipedia.org/w/index.php?title=File:Valorous_Unit_Award_ribbon.svg *License*: Public Domain *Contributors*: user:Ipankonin

File:Meritorious Unit Commendation ribbon.svg *Source*: http://en.wikipedia.org/w/index.php?title=File:Meritorious_Unit_Commendation_ribbon.svg *License*: Public Domain *Contributors*: user:Ipankonin

File:Army Good Conduct ribbon.svg *Source*: http://en.wikipedia.org/w/index.php?title=File:Army_Good_Conduct_ribbon.svg *License*: Public Domain *Contributors*: US Army

File:AFEMRib.svg *Source*: http://en.wikipedia.org/w/index.php?title=File:AFEMRib.svg *License*: GNU Free Documentation License *Contributors*: user:Shazz

File:Armed Forces Reserve Medal ribbon.png *Source*: http://en.wikipedia.org/w/index.php?title=File:Armed_Forces_Reserve_Medal_ribbon.png *License*: Public Domain *Contributors*: Darz Mol, FieldMarine

File:Vietnam Campaign Medal ribbon.png *Source*: http://en.wikipedia.org/w/index.php?title=File:Vietnam_Campaign_Medal_ribbon.png *License*: Public Domain *Contributors*: Original uploader was PalawanOz at en.wikipedia

File:Flickr - The U.S. Army - Medal of Honor, Maj. Bruce Crandall.jpg *Source*: http://en.wikipedia.org/w/index.php?title=File:Flickr_-_The_U.S._Army_-_Medal_of_Honor,_Maj._Bruce_Crandall.jpg *License*: Public Domain *Contributors*: The U.S. Army

File:Ed freeman 2001.jpg *Source*: http://en.wikipedia.org/w/index.php?title=File:Ed_freeman_2001.jpg *License*: Public Domain *Contributors*: Original uploader was Nv8200p at en.wikipedia

File:Moh army mil.jpg *Source*: http://en.wikipedia.org/w/index.php?title=File:Moh_army_mil.jpg *License*: Public Domain *Contributors*: CORNELIUSSEON, Jwillbur

File:Distinguished Flying Cross ribbon.svg *Source*: http://en.wikipedia.org/w/index.php?title=File:Distinguished_Flying_Cross_ribbon.svg *License*: Public Domain *Contributors*: user:Ipankonin

Image:PD-icon.svg *Source*: http://en.wikipedia.org/w/index.php?title=File:PD-icon.svg *License*: Public Domain *Contributors*: User:Duesentrieb, User:Rfl

CPSIA information can be obtained at www.ICGtesting.com
Printed in the USA
LVOW120453120612

285716LV00003B/30/P